Bright Lights Dark Deeds : The True Story of Marjorie Orbin

Samantha Reese

Published by Trellis Publishing, 2021.

While every precaution has been taken in the preparation of this book, the publisher assumes no responsibility for errors or omissions, or for damages resulting from the use of the information contained herein.

BRIGHT LIGHTS DARK DEEDS : THE TRUE STORY OF MARJORIE ORBIN

First edition. July 9, 2021.

Copyright © 2021 Samantha Reese.

ISBN: 979-8224014293

Written by Samantha Reese.

SELECTED STORIES
by Poppy Z. Brite
Collection – eBook Edition
February 2016

THE HITCHHIKING EFFECT
by Gene O'Neill
Collection – eBook Edition
February 2016

INDEPENDENT LEGIONS PUBLISHING
Via Virgilio, 10 – TRIESTE (ITALY)
+39 040 9776602
www.independentlegions.com
independent.legions@aol.com

BRIGHT LIGHTS, DARK DEEDS : THE TRUE STORY OF MARJORIE ORBIN

SAMANTHA REESE

Marjorie Ann Orbin: Bright Lights, Dark Deeds

There is nothing more appealing than a murder that has all the right elements. There needs to be a pretty girl with sex appeal, a lot of money, and, of course, someone else to blame. There are a lot of reasons to kill someone. Some people do it out of hatred. Some people do it for personal advancement. Some people do it simply because they are evil people. No one will ever be certain if or why this particular murder occurred, but the speculation around it would affect the family and friends of the victim for years after the event. This is a case out of Phoenix, Arizona about a man who fell in love with a Vegas Showgirl.

The Character of Marjorie

Marjorie Ann Orbin was born in Florida on October 29, 1961. She was just eighteen years old when doctors informed her that she would never have children. Very little is known about her life before that significant moment, a defining moment really for her, and one that would shape the course of the rest of her years.

Marjorie had always been pretty and athletic. She used these two traits; along with the fact that she now knew she could never have children to pursue a career as a dancer. With essentially nothing to lose she adopted a 'work hard, play hard' type attitude towards life and she lived each day to the fullest. She never wanted to miss an opportunity.

And it was no surprise that she took this mentality into all aspects of her life, including her love life. As she could not have children, Marjorie was probably a little more cavalier than most with her love life. She went through many relationships and each one was as intense as the next. Every man she met held the potential to be prince charming in her eyes and she pursued these men with the intent of fostering a long term and meaningful relationship each time. She would never let a chance at true love pass her by.

At some point in time in between her relationships with various men she became a stripper as a career choice. Marjorie said in a later interview, "I never felt disrespected and I never did anything that I would be afraid to tell my mother". During her time at one of these strip clubs Marjorie became close with one of the regulars.

This was the first time that she met twenty-six year old Jay Orbin. He was a regular at her strip club and he pursued Marjorie heavily. They went out on a date and he wined and dined her, but at twenty-four, Marjorie had her eyes set on a more glamorous life than what Jay Orbin could offer her. So the two went their separate ways and Marjorie continued her pursuit of the life of her dreams.

Money and Fame

Marjorie went returned to Florida where she'd grown up and reconnected with a man who could get her to her life in the spotlight. His name was Michael J. Peter and Marjorie had known him since she was seventeen years old.

She used this long lasting friendship as leverage and when she went back to Florida she began to work for him. Michael J. Peter was a multi-millionaire who created upscale strip clubs around the world. She travelled all around the world with him for work and in return he made Marjorie his chief dancer and choreographer in his clubs. He even gave Marjorie a lead role in his movie "No More Dirty Deals".

Marjorie and Michael dated for several years and were engaged, but the industry is hard for couples, especially when you are with a man like Michael who lives in the spotlight surrounded by beautiful women. Marjorie was never fully comfortable with the number of women that threw themselves at Michael. She had always had a jealous bone and eventually it just became too much for her to handle. It was this fact that eventually led to their breakup and Marjorie took her talents back to Las Vegas.

Full Circle

In 1993 a travelling salesman from Phoenix called on Marjorie while she was working at a Vegas Strip club. It was Jay Orbin. Marjorie hadn't seen him in ten years, but apparently he hadn't forgotten about her. Jay indicated that he was travelling through Vegas and he'd seen a billboard with Marjorie's picture on it. He wanted to know if she had any interest in getting a drink. She agreed to have a drink with him and they talked all night until the sun came up, getting drinks and snacks at different locations.

Jay headed on to Phoenix the next day but their relationship continued past that magical night of drinks until dawn. "People liked to paint us as polar opposites," Marjorie said in a later interview, "but we really weren't. We had the exact same ideals."

The main one of these ideals was having children. Marjorie had always wanted to have children, even though she'd been told it would never happen. And Jay had always wanted a wife and a child. It would seem like these two would be incompatible based on that one factor, but Jay was determined to have Marjorie in his life and he was determined to do whatever it took to get her there and build the life he wanted with her.

Jay, who at that point in his life was the successful owner of a Native American art store, offered to pay for fertility treatments for Marjorie if she agreed to marry him and move to Phoenix with him. It was quite the offer and one that Marjorie was likely not going to get from anyone else. And there was nothing she wanted more in life than to have a child, it was her one unrealized dream. She'd had her fame and fortune, she'd had her time in the spotlight, but she'd never had her chance to be a mother. And there was Jay offering her that opportunity, holding it like a carrot on a stick.

Joanne Orbin, Jay's mother, wasn't so certain that Marjorie was the girl for her son. She wasn't pleased with the whole situation in the least. Joanne wasn't impressed with Marjorie. Sure, she was beautiful, but not nearly as beautiful as she seemed to think she was. Marjorie believed that Joanne was jealous of the attention that Jay paid to her and the way he was so devoted to her. Needless to say, the two women did not get along.

Regardless of his mother's opinion, the happy couple eloped at the Little White Wedding Chapel in Laws Vegas. Jay's brother, Jake Orbin, came to visit a few month's later to check on his brother and too meet his new sister-in-law. Jake saw Marjorie as the perfect housewife. As far as he saw she took care of everything around the house and made all the meals. He had no complaints to make about her as a person or as a partner for his brother.

However, the fertility treatments were taking a toll on Marjorie. They often made Marjorie ill and rundown. However, she was more than willing to trade the side effects for the chance to have a child. And finally it happened, after a long battle with the treatments. Marjorie gave birth to their son, Noah, their miracle baby.

For all intents and purposes they seemed like the perfect family. Marjorie spent ten years in Phoenix being a wife, a mom, and a business partner. They were a happy little family, but things can't always remain as they were. And things changed very quickly for the Orbins and they took a sharp turn for the worst.

A Missing Husband

The happy life of the Orbin family all ended in September of 2004. According to Marjorie, "an unforeseen, tragic incident that I came upon after the fact caused the death of Jay Orbin". Marjorie claimed in an interview five years after the fact that she is not responsible for her husband's death, but that she knows who is. Still, the facts around his disappearance and death remain mysterious.

On August 26, 2004 the family all attended Noah's birthday party and without being aware of it at the time, this would be the last occassion that Jay Orbin would see his son. Shortly after the birthday party ended, Jay hit the road for a sales trip to Florida. The trip carried a dark cloud with it from the start, literally, as Hurricane Francis was currently devastating the state of Florida. This made Jay decided to cut his losses and head home before he even made it all the way.

On September 8, 2004 Joanna called her son to wish him happy birthday, his 45th birthday in fact. He was just driving into Phoenix at that time on his way back from his failed sales trip. He told his mother that he would talk to her later, but they never spoke to him again. This was extremely unlike Jay. When a week went by Joanna became frantic, but Marjorie was dismissive of her worry much like she was dismissive of everything when it came to her mother-in-law.

Marjorie told everyone that Jay had come back from Florida and then headed out on another sales trip immediately after. She made it very clear that there was no reason to worry about her husband's absence or the fact that he wasn't returning calls. Another week passed and Jay's desperate friends and family convinced Marjorie to call the police.

Detective Jan Butcher of the missing person's unit took on the case at that point. Jan said, "I asked [Marjorie] to provide me with the information on the license plate of the vehicle Jay was driving. She said she'd call me back and she never did, so that was a little bit odd." Marjorie's reluctance to openly cooperate with the investigation quickly made her a target for the investigation.

On September 28th Detective Butcher left three messages before Marjorie finally called back. Detective Butcher recorded the conversation that the two of them had. During the conversation Marjorie indicated that her and Jay were no longer married and that they had divorced for tax reasons. Detective Butcher expressed her concern over Marjorie's lack of cooperation in the investigation to find her husband. This opinion was not taken well by Marjorie.

Marjorie indicated that just because she wasn't being hysterical like everyone else, didn't mean she wasn't doing anything. And Detective Butcher quickly confirmed that she was in fact doing something. She was spending a good portion of Jay's money. She spent $45 000 from his business account and she purchased a $12 000 baby grand piano. Marjorie justified her expensive purchases by stating she was in a daze, confused over the loss of her husband. She indicated that her actions didn't really make sense, but that was okay in her opinion.

When Detective Butcher asked Marjorie to take a polygraph she became very defensive and began to speak to someone in the house with her while on the phone with the detective. It turned out that the other individual was Marjorie's boyfriend, Larry Weisberg. She was involved with a production manager she'd met at the gym. How long the relationship had been going on was unclear, but there was definitely more to the story than just a missing husband now. There was a love triangle forming and growing incentive to make Jay Orbin leave the picture.

After hearing the obscenity filled phone call that she had with Marjorie and Larry, Detective Butcher acquired a search warrant and had SWAT deliver it to the Orbin household. SWAT raided the house and was confronted by Larry Weisberg. He didn't move when requested so one SWAT member tased him and he received a facial injury as well. Marjorie stated later that she was not concerned with what happened to Larry during the raid, she was concerned about the fact that the SWAT team raiding the house might scare her son.

The SWAT team made no arrests when they raided the house; however the raid turned up some interesting new evidence. They found Jay Orbin's checkbook that he always takes with him when he went on sales trips and numerous credit cards that he would also travel with. It was clear that Jay had returned to the house after his trip to Florida and then never left again on another sales trip. This had Detective Butcher thinking that it was no longer a missing person's case and that it was a homicide investigation.

A Rubbermaid Grave

On October 23, 2004 a transient man came across a container in the desert wrapped in heavy black plastic only to discover the torso of a body. All of the internal organs were missing and if that was not bad enough his arms, legs and head were also cut off.

It was six weeks after he went missing, that police believed that they found Jay Orbin. "As we walked up you could smell the death in the air. Once you smell it you know what it is for the rest of your life," said Detective David Barnes, who was called to the scene. He went on to say "It was the first time I'd ever seen anything like that, where it's just a piece of a body."

They found a torso, a wad of cash, and a spent bullet all packed inside a Rubbermaid coffin in the desert. A DNA test later confirmed what Joanna Orbin already feared, her son was dead. And even worse, someone had abandoned him in the desert, desecrated his body, and stuffed him in a Rubbermaid.

The murder investigation began where the missing person's investigation had ended, with one person: Marjorie Orbin. Jay's body had been found less than a mile from his own home and the detectives believed that Marjorie had placed Jay's body so close to her own home so that it would be found, because without a body she had no claim to Jay's estate. And as far as anyone could tell from her actions up until that point, it was all about the money for Marjorie. As far as anyone could tell, it had always been about the money for Marjorie.

Three weeks after finding Jay's body the police detained Marjorie for forging Jay's signature at a Circuit City store. Marjorie indicated that she was just trying to purchase a computer to replace one that had been confiscated during the police raid so that she could continue to run the business and bring revenue into the home. The detective's questioning her quickly steered the conversation from check fraud to murder as they continue to interrogate her.

Detective Barnes took over the questioning at this point and confronted Marjorie with a photo that she'd never seen before. It is an image of Jay's butchered torso. She turned away from the image and acted shocked. For all intents and purposes she seemed appalled that the detective would show her such an image.

They arrested her for credit card fraud, but she was released later that evening. However, the evidence against her continued to mount. Investigators found receipts for mops and cleaning products purchased the day after Jay went missing. It was clear that Marjorie had acid washed the garage floor and then poxy coated the floor recently. This process had completely erased any evidence of blood that they could have found in the garage making it impossible to link the garage as a potential murder scene.

However, they did locate surveillance footage from inside the Lowe's hardware store that was fairly damning. On September 10, 2004, two days after Jay went missing Marjorie is caught on camera purchasing two Rubbermaid containers and other assorted items with Jay Orbin's American Express card. These are the same containers that Jay's body was later found in. It was as much of a smoking gun as the police were going to get at that point.

Still, Marjorie continued to insist that the gun was pointed at the wrong person. "I trusted someone that I should not have and I aided and abetted someone that I should not have," Marjorie said later.

Larry Weisberg was also a person of interest in the case. The police found some of his clothing in Jay Orbin's house and it was clear that he had a fairly established relationship with Marjorie. They were interested to know who he was and what his involvement was in the whole matter. The detectives believed that Larry and Marjorie were in a developed relationship and that it was a potential motive for the murder. When the police searched Larry's car and home they found that Larry had remote access to Jay's garage. It was not exactly damning evidence, but it was something.

Larry could have been the one responsible for killing Jay; however, all of the evidence pointed towards Marjorie and it seemed that the police were really only interested in looking at her.

The Arrest of A Showgirl

On December 6, 2004, six weeks after the discovery of Jay Orbin's dismembered body Marjorie Orbin was arrested. She was arrested in her house in front of her child and charged with the murder of Jay Orbin. Noah Orbin was sent to live with Jay's brother Jake and Larry Weisberg was offered use immunity. This essentially meant that what he said to the police could not be used against him in court.

Five Years of Silence

Despite her lawyer's opposition to this deal, Marjorie did not speak out against it. She later claimed it was because of threats that had been made against her by Larry. She indicated that she had been threatened and that the life of her son had been threatened as well. She said that the message had been clear: "if you tell the police that I committed this crime I will kill your son".

Marjorie claimed that Larry Weisberg was responsible for Jay Orbin's death. However, it is not until 5 years after the fact that she spoke out about this. She claimed it was due to the threats made against her son's life. She claimed that Larry shot Jay and that Noah was crying and screaming and Larry said, "it's just that easy to snap his scrawny neck if you don't do as you're told". She had to keep her mouth shut and go along with the story. She also admits to helping Larry cover up the murder, but she was adamant that she was not responsible for Jay's death.

Marjorie approached her trial date almost five years after her original imprisonment. She knew that this trial could result in her being sentenced to death, but she refused to take a plea deal. She refused to let her son believe that she is responsible for his father's death.

Trina Kay, the prosecution, worked hard during the trial to paint the picture of Marjorie as nothing more than a stripper who used men for their money. She made sure to indicate that Larry Weisberg was nothing more than just another boy-toy in a long history of men for Marjorie. Kay spun a narrative around the concept that Marjorie hated

Jay, that he disgusted her, and that she wanted him dead so that she could have his money. It was about nothing more than sex and money when it came to Marjorie. That was the story that Kay pushed to the jury.

Jay's body was cut into pieces using a jigsaw. The investigators never found the gun or the saw, but the police do have the footage of Marjorie purchasing the items. Kay made sure to make this connection clear to the jury as well.

Most damning, however, was the use of Sophia Johnson, Marjorie's former cellmate, who was put on the stand by the prosecution. She only acted to solidify their case against Marjorie. She was able to speak about incidents where Marjorie would go on tangents about things about Jay that were disgusting. She offered several short narratives that built on the prosecutions case.

"He was shot, frozen, de-thawed, and his arms, legs, and head were cut off," says Sophia reciting what she'd been told by Marjorie.

Larry also took the stand and painted a picture of Marjorie as a seductress who used him for his body. He also indicated that he had no clue what had happened to Jay Orbin. He went on to indicate that he had no involvement in the murder of Jay Orbin. He made a very believable witness.

The defense tried to discredit Larry in the cross examination, painting him as a dishonest man and a man crazy enough to take on a SWAT team. They indicated that he was angry enough to swear at police over the telephone while Marjorie was on the phone with them. And they made sure to point out that he was strong enough to dispose of a 280-pound man.

Detective Barnes even began to question whether or not Larry could be responsible for this murder at this point in time. There had been evidence that could have implicated Larry that was never tested by the Phoenix crime lab. There were hairs that were found on the tub that were never tested. They could have belonged to Marjorie or to

Larry. However, the crime lab refused to test the hairs when asked by the detective.

Detective Barnes said, "I know for a fact that Marjorie is involved. I don't know for a fact that Larry was involved. Is it possible? I think it is possible, but everything that we looked at and everything that we were allowed to test eliminated Larry".

Two hairs that were tested did not match Larry or Marjorie, and several hairs remained untested by the crime lab. Trina Kay was confident in the evidence they had for the trial. None of the items taken from Larry's home implicated him in any way in the murder of Jay Orbin. All of the evidence pointed towards Marjorie, just like it always had.

Three months into the trial Detective Barnes was placed on leave for what Phoenix police called "harassment". Barnes believed that his leave had more to do with his criticism of the crime lab in this case and several other cases than any form of actual harassment. Regardless, he was shut down from pursuing the matter further.

As the trial continued, Michael J Peter, Marjorie's former boss and boyfriend, spoke up on her behalf. He described a completely different person than the one that the prosecution had indicated. He stated that Marjorie was a kind and gentle person incapable of killing a spider let alone of hurting a person. Michael even stated that he had offered to support Marjorie and Noah if she would leave Jay and come back to him. However, he states that Marjorie said, "Jay is a good man and I would never take the father from the child or the child from the father".

The defence advised Marjorie not to take the stand. They made it clear to her that the prosecution has no eyewitness, no forensic evidence, and no murder weapon. The defense is confident at that point that Marjorie could win the case. The lawyers told Marjorie that the prosecution had not proven things beyond a reasonable doubt and therefore the jury could not convict her. So she remained seated and did not take the stand. This is a decision that she would forever question.

The trial was eight months long in its total process; however the jury only deliberated for seven hours in order to decide the outcome of Marjorie Ann Orbin's life. The jury came back to find Marjorie guilty unanimously. Marjorie was sentenced to life in prison on October 1, 2009. The jurors ruled against the death penalty and instead opted for life imprisonment without the possibility of parole. She is currently serving out her life sentence at the Arizona State Prison Complex in Perryville.

A DEADLY INTERNET LOVE TRIANGLE

14

MICHELLE BLUE

Chapter 1

Sharee Miller was a gorgeous, single mother-of-three when she met her husband Bruce Miller. At the time, she was in her early twenties, broke, and weeks away from being homeless.

The couple initially met when Sharee began working at Bruce's automobile scrap yard as a bookkeeper. After only three months, Sharee moved herself and her three kids into Bruce's house and they quickly became a family. Bruce gave Sharee a sense of stability she had never experienced and Sharee was kind, caring, and loving to Bruce.

After only a few more months, the couple married. Domestic bliss loomed on the horizon.

But six months later, Bruce was dead.

Initially, the events that led to Bruce's death were a complete mystery to police until a former homicide detective miles away shot himself in the head and left behind a briefcase of evidence.

How these two deaths were connected would shock police, and lead to one of the most infamous crimes in America.

Chapter 2

Sharee Miller, then Sharee Kitley, was born on October 13, 1971, in Flint, Michigan.

At the time, Flint was a powerhouse of economic growth largely due to the GM Buick and Chevrolet factories that operated in the city. General Motor's history was largely intertwined with Flint—the company's founder had formed the GM company in Flint in 1908. The GM factories in Flint were also the setting of the and iconic 1936-37 Sit-Down Strike—the strike that led to the creation of the United Auto Worker's union.

Flint made money because Flint made cars.

However, the Kitley family did not drink from the city's pool of wealth. They lived on the town's outskirts, a rough working-class neighborhood. They're home was a single-wide trailer smack-dab in the center of a tornado's playground. Sharee was an only child, she was the sole receiver of her parent's attention, but this attention was not desired by Sharee. Sharee's parents fought often, and when they were finished fighting with each other, they'd fight with Sharee.

In mid 80's, when Sharee was in her early teens, GM Motors closed its factories' doors in Flint. The city quickly fell to pieces, ramshackle remains of the auto empire it had once been. The city fell into a deep depression.

As she watched her hometown descend into ruins, Sharee decided to leave her toxic home for good. At the age of 16, Sharee moved in with her boyfriend at the time, and when that ended she couched surfed and work a variety of dead-end jobs, most of which only lasted a few months.

When she was 18, Sharee found herself pregnant and married to an abusive husband. The two shared a home in yet another low-income project in another rough neighborhood left in the dust of Flint's ruined automobile empire. Sharee watched her childhood repeat itself in front of her own eyes, but this time, it was her first-born son who held the starring role of the helpless child. Sharee ended the marriage after she caught her spouse physically abusing the young boy. It was one of the only lines Sharee drew in the sand—you did not harm her children.

Although Sharee took this brave step towards saving her son, history often repeated itself throughout her life. Two more failed attempts at finding a soulmate yielded two more children for the young woman. The single mother-of-three now resorted to frequently moving from low-income house to low-income house and took any odd job she could find—anything to keep her kids off the street.

Chapter 3

In 1997, Sharee was a single mother-of-three who was three breaths and an electricity bill away from being homeless. During an attempt to keep her kids safe and housed, Sharee took a job as a bookkeeper with B&D Auto, a small auto scrapyard that fit right in in the middle of Flint's automobile history.

Sharee had been hired despite having little-to-no experience keeping books in the past. She had convinced the boss, Bruce Miller, that she was hard-working, a fast learner, and desperate for a paycheque. And that seemed to be enough. That and the fact that Sharee was a stunner. Her bright blonde hair only drew more attention to her enrapturing icy blue eyes.

Bruce was a kind and generous soul. He took a chance on Sharee and it seemed to pay off. Only a few months after Sharee had begun working at the scrapyard, she and Bruce moved their relationship from the office to the bedroom. It wasn't long before Sharee and her three kids moved in with Bruce. The four now lived in a stable, secure home for the first time in any of their lives.

Bruce and Sharee married only months after they first met. Bruce, who has twenty-one his new bride's senior, thought he had finally found the perfect wife. Young, sexy, and loving. It was all he had ever wanted.

Her new life with Bruce was also a dream come true for Sharee. She had finally found a man that treated her right, and in him, she also found security. Ten years ago, she had left her own unhappy parents and embarked on a life of poverty and abuse. Now, she was sitting in the living room of a big house, watching her children—the true loves of her life—swimming in Bruce's above-ground pool. It was the idyllic life she never thought she could have.

But idyllicism did not suit Sharee.

Chapter 4

While Sharee lived the life she had always wanted for herself and her kids, Bruce's own family began to have doubts behind Sharee's motives.

Initially, Bruce's family took no issue with the fact that Bruce's wife was so young. The couple looked so happy and in love, they formed a perfect family. Bruce was even in the process of adopting Sharee's three boys. But things slowly began to change.

Sharee began to take advantage of her new wealth. She no longer worked at the scrapyard but began selling Mary Kay Cosmetics to other bored housewives instead. She began spending every penny of her earnings, and a whole lot more of Bruce's, on luxuries she had never been presented with before. She bought expensive jewelry and clothes, she got her first credit card plus a few more, and she bought an expensive computer for the home.

Bruce, however, did not partake in his family's worries. He was as happy as ever the day Jerry Cassaday stepped into his office and shot him square in the chest. Bruce understood Sharee's desire to buy things, he enjoyed watching her be careless with money for the first time in her life. And most of all, Bruce was proud that she began selling cosmetics door-to-door. An entrepreneur himself, he found Sharee's new profession to be ambitious. Bold. He had no qualms when Sharee brought home expensive dress after expensive dress, and he was nothing but proud when she showed him the computer she claimed was to help her keep track of all her sales.

If you had asked Bruce, he would have said the couple was as happy as could be.

Sharee, evidently, was not happy. Although she was pleased with the security her marriage to Bruce brought, she was bored. She was living the life of a housewife and simply got restless. She started going online and frequenting chat rooms where she could talk to strangers and meet new men. She could talk to these new men and Bruce would be none the wiser.

It was the perfect situation for Sharee. She got to keep the stable home life she knew she needed while engaging in the excitement of meeting new singles and falling in love without the latter threatening the first. In short, she got to have her cake and eat it too.

But this quickly fell apart. Soon, the satisfaction Sharee got from speaking to these men online began to fade. She needed more. She wanted to meet these men, feel their touch. This yearning was fresh in her mind the day she met Jerry Cassaday.

Chapter 5

Jerry Cassaday was working as a pit boss in a Reno casino. Before that, he had been a homicide detective and police officer for the Marshall Police Department and the Cass County Sheriff's Department. He began frequenting online chat rooms after his wife left him. He was lonely and had always wanted a family. He went online hoping to find companionship and an honest connection with a beautiful woman. Instead, he found Sharee Miller.

The two hit it off immediately. For Cassaday, it was love at first sight. He was enraptured by the blue-eyed blonde-haired twenty-something-year-old. There was only one problem: Sharee lived in Flint, Michigan and Cassaday was stuck in Reno, Nevada. They had no way to meet without arousing the suspicions of Sharee's husband Bruce until the perfect opportunity arose—a Mary Kay Cosmetics conference was announced. The location? None other than Reno, Nevada.

Sharee jumped at this opportunity to meet Cassaday in person and the spark they had struck up online burst into flames when they met in person. The two spent every free minute they had together, and Sharee even accompanied Cassaday to work. She would sit at his table and play hands of blackjack. When Cassaday finished for the night, the two would go back to Sharee's hotel room.

While Sharee was honest about being married at the time, she altered many details about her life in Flint to her favor. It was all part of the fantasy she had built up for herself online. Sharee told Cassaday that her husband was a high-ranking member of the mafia who frequently beat her and mistreated her children. They weren't in love, she was just too afraid to leave. Cassaday, who was in his mid 30's at the time, had always wanted a family and was aghast when Sharee told him the details about how her current husband treated herself and her kids. Little did he know it was all a lie.

The picture Sharee painted of her husband Bruce was so far away from the handsome, family-orientated business man that he really was. She wasn't describing reality, she was describing a fantasy. And Cassaday had bought it.

After Sharee inevitably left her new lover behind to return home to Flint, Sharee kept up their flame by sending numerous naked photos by email to Cassaday. They kept in constant touch through emails and instant messages. The two kept in touch so frequently that members of Bruce's family could later recall him complaining about the amount of time Sharee began to spend on her new computer. He knew something was up, he just wasn't sure what.

Sharee continued to build on the fantasy she had created with Cassaday. As well as nude photos, she would send him photos of herself covered in bruise-coloured makeup claiming they were from Bruce. On one special occasion, she went old school and snail-mailed Cassaday a tape labeled For Jerry's Eyes Only...

As Sharee fell deeper into the rabbit hole she had dug, two things became clear to her: the first, Cassaday was completely and utterly under her control, the second, she liked her new fantasy more than her real marriage.

Chapter 6

Sharee Miller's life had taken such a turn from her younger years. She had a stable life, a happy home, and a loving husband. But somehow, this was no longer enough for Sharee. Addicted to the danger of the unknown, Sharee had become bored in her easy marriage. She craved more.

She found the perfect path out of her marriage in Jerry Cassaday. Initially, the thrill of an affair was enough for her, but this eventually grew old—especially when her affair became online only.

Usually, when someone grows tired of their online relationship, they break up with their partner and cease communications. This was not the case with Sharee and Jerry Cassaday. When Sharee grew tired of her online affair with Cassaday she did not stop communications—she increased them. Although she had fallen out of love with the ex-homicide detective, she still needed him for one very specific purpose. He was going to kill her husband for her.

Cassaday had fallen madly in love with Sharee. He believed she was married to an abusive husband who has a high-ranking mafia player. He feared for his beautiful girlfriend and would do almost anything to protect her. Almost wasn't good enough for Sharee though. Sharee was going to use Cassaday to get out of her marriage, and to do so, she was going to have to make him mad first. Mad enough to kill.

Sharee's plan seemed foolproof. Bruce, her husband, was alone at his auto scrapyard a lot, and he always carried a large amount of cash on him, roughly $2000, in order to make change for his customers. Sharee saw this as the perfect opportunity. Someone could easily kill Bruce at his work with no witnesses, and better yet, if they took the cash on him, it would look like a robbery-gone-wrong. This would inevitably point police away from herself. All she needed was someone to pull the trigger.

Chapter 7

At some point during their online relationship, Sharee realized that she had Cassaday wrapped around her finger. She had seduced him in online and in-person and had maintained this enrapturement through sending him endless emails and seductive videos. Sharee began to use this power she had over Cassaday to make him angry. She had already painted her kind, gentle husband to be an abusive mafia man, but she needed more.

About a month after meeting with Cassaday in person, Sharee went to her local pharmacy and purchased a pregnancy test. She knew she wasn't pregnant—she had had her tubes tied after the birth of her third son—but she needed Cassaday to think she was. She went home, took photos of herself with her stomach pushed out, and sent them to Cassaday along with photos of the pregnancy test, which she had drawn lines on so it appeared to be a positive test. To make the lie seem more real, she also sent an image of her third child's sonograms.

I'm pregnant, she wrote Cassaday, with your first children. Twins.

A few weeks later, Sharee sent Cassaday more pictures of her stomach. This time, however, she coated her belly in blue and purple makeup first.

He killed our beautiful babies was the message sent along with the photos.

Cassaday was devastated, his lover's abusive husband had just taken from the world what he thought would be his opportunity to have a normal life with the woman he loved. He fell into a severe state of depression. Cassaday could not take the news. He could no longer watch the woman he loved destroyed by her own oppressive husband. No. He was coming to town to free Sharee and finally have the family he'd always wanted.

Sharee was ecstatic. Through one later-debated series of instant messages, Sharee slowly revealed her perfect plan on how Cassaday should murder Bruce. The whole of Sharee's plan was summed up in only a few damning sentences.

I'll call Bruce at 5pm and tell him to call me when he's leaving. Pull up to the left side of the building, right to the door. He'll be at the desk inside. Take his wallet. Take the whole thing.

Chapter 8

On November 8, 1999, Jerry Cassaday drove from Reno to Flint to kill the man he thought killed his twin babies and repeatedly beat the love of his life.

He followed Sharee's instructions to the word. At 5pm he pulled up to Bruce Miller's auto scrapyard, went inside, shot Bruce in the chest, and took Bruce's wallet. Bruce was on the phone with Sharee at the time, just as she had planned. Sharee had chosen to listen to her husband die.

Cassaday's experience as a homicide detective meant that he could commit the crime without leaving forensic evidence behind. He left the scrapyard office without leaving a single finger or footprint and took Bruce's wallet without ripping the pocket, a general characteristic of a rushed robbery. Investigators were also unable to recover any trace fibers or hairs from the scene or Bruce's body.

After committing the crime he had spent the majority of his life solving, Cassaday turned his car around and headed straight back to Nevada.

Chapter 9

A few hours after listening to her lover shoot her husband, Sharee called her brother-in-law Chuck Miller. She frantically told him that Bruce was missing, he hadn't come home for dinner and his work phone wasn't working. She convinced Chuck to drive out to the scrapyard to check on his brother.

When Chuck arrived, he was affronted with a horrible scene—Bruce was laying face down on the ground dead from a gunshot wound to his chest. His telephone receiver was on the ground next to his face. Within an hour, a full team of homicide investigators were on the scene.

Due to the lack of physical evidence at the scene, investigator's initially had little to go on. The main motive appeared to be robbery, just another day in Flint.

Sharee was brought in for questioning but was never suspected by police. She had been at home all day with her children and several friends. They simply wanted to ask her if she had any idea of who would want her husband dead, and Sharee was prepared for this.

Sharee told detectives that one of her former boyfriends John Hutchinson had owed Bruce several thousands of dollars. Bruce and

Hutchinson had several arguments about this as well as the tumultuous state of Sharee and Hutchinson's former relationship.

Hutchison unluckily had no solid alibi. He quickly emerged as the key suspect in Bruce's murder.

To make things worse for Hutchinson, he had agreed to take a lie-detector test to prove his innocence, but the examination did not go smoothly. In the middle of the test Hutchinson collapsed and ended up going to the hospital. Not only had he failed the few questions he had been asked, but he was so clearly stressed about the test that he had physical symptoms.

The general feeling amongst investigators was that Hutchinson had killed Bruce, they just couldn't prove it. While his autopsy revealed that Bruce had been shot by a 20 gauge shotgun, Hutchinson did not own this type of gun and investigators failed to find one during a search of his home.

Eventually, much to Sharee's delight, the case went cold. It wasn't until a seemingly unrelated suicide miles away took place before police had any reason to suspect Sharee.

Chapter 10

After he returned to his home in Reno, Jerry Cassaday expected his relationship with Sharee Miller to continue as usual. He believed that they would continue to date long-distance until the murder investigation cooled down. Then, Sharee would begin a new life in Reno with Cassaday.

This, however, was not the case.

Sharee barely contacted Cassaday after the death of her husband. She didn't initiate any conversations and stopped replying to his emails altogether. Cassaday, still deep in the world of lies Sharee had created, began to panic.

A few weeks after killing her husband, Cassaday decided to pay Sharee a visit to make sure she was doing okay. When he arrived at her home in Flint, his world fell apart.

Sharee was at home with her three kids and a new boyfriend.

She had double-crossed Cassaday within weeks of the murder. Cassaday instantly returned to the state of depression he had been in when he believed that Bruce had killed his baby twins-to-be.

Sharee and Cassaday never spoke again, and Sharee had almost entirely forgot about her ex-lover when police started knocking on her door again.

Chapter 11

Seven hundred miles away from Sharee and Flint, in Kansas City, Missouri, Jerry Cassaday was found dead in his home, a gun in his hand, Bible in his lap, shot in the head. Cassaday could not live with the crimes he had committed for love, especially knowing that the love he felt wasn't real. It was too much for him.

Before he killed himself, Cassaday took measures to ensure his death would be connected back to Sharee and Bruce Miller's murder. Next to his body, police found his open briefcase which contained his suicide note addressed to his parents and a printed transcript of extensive instant messaging conversations. Outside in the trash, investigators also found a scandalous video of a young woman dancing naked addressed directly to Jerry.

Police showed clips of this video to Jerry's neighbors in order to identify the woman dancing. Several neighbors were able to identify Jerry's online girlfriend Sharee, who lived in Flint. When Kansas City police called the Flint sheriff's office to get more information about Sharee, Flint police were astounded. They instantly knew they had been duped by the blonde, beautiful widow.

When she was identified by Kansas City police, Sharee was immediately connected not only to Cassaday's suicide but also back to her ex-husband Bruce's murder. In his suicide note, Cassaday revealed that he had been the one to kill Bruce. Sadly, it was evident that he still believed many of the lies Sharee had told him. He stated in his note that he had to do it, Bruce had killed his children and that was something he couldn't let go. Even if it meant destroying his own life in the process.

He also described Sharee's role in the murder plot. He stated that she had encouraged him to commit the murder and helped him plan it. He could not have done it without her help. And he had provided investigators with the transcripts to prove it.

Sharee miller was brought in for questioning where she claimed she did not even know Jerry Cassaday. She stuck to this story until police revealed that they had the tape of her dancing, addressed in her handwriting as being For Jerry's Eyes Only. After this, she was forced to change her story. It was undisputable evidence that they had had a relationship.

Sharee then told police she had met Jerry in a computer chatroom while just messing around, trying to figure out something new to do. Computer forensic experts then confiscated both Sharee and Cassaday's computers. What they found inside answered some important questions but raised many others.

Investigators easily found their way into Sharee and Cassaday's private online conversations. They found incriminating evidence on Jerry's computer—the online copy of the instant messaging conversation in which Cassaday and Sharee discussed Bruce's murder. When they confronted Sharee with these messages, she had a planned response: Cassaday was framing her.

Sharee told investigators that in the triangle of herself, her ex-husband Bruce, and Jerry Cassaday, Cassaday was the scorned lover. After she got bored with her online affair, she tried to cut contact with Cassaday, but he wouldn't let her. She claimed that Cassaday had forged the messages to implicate her in something she had never been apart of. Investigators thought that this claim was far-fetched, so they reached out to AOL, the company that hosted the instant messaging service Cassaday and Sharee used to communicate. Surprisingly, AOL took Sharee's side on the issue—it was possible for the messages to have been forged.

Investigators were now tasked with proving the legitimacy of the instant messages that showed Sharee had helped plan Bruce's murder with Cassaday. Under court order, AOL released information about Sharee and Jerry's computer activity. They confirmed that both Jerry and Sharee had been online and logged into the AOL service the same day at the same time for the same length of time as the instant message indicated. Police also found handwritten notes copied in Sharee's writing that listed information found in the messages. If they had been forged, Sharee would not have known this information in order to write it down.

Sharee was now trapped. Although she continued to maintain her innocence, investigators continued to find more and more damning evidence against Sharee.

Sharee had taken steps to cover her online footprints. A day and a half after the death of her husband she had called AOL to change her first name, last name, and her address. After she learned of the suicide of Jerry Cassaday, she did the same thing again. She was clearly worried about the content of her online messages being traced back to her.

Once investigators had confirmed the legitimacy of the messages, they were able to read the diary of Sharee's relationship with Cassaday. They were able to see how she was able to bring Cassaday to a boil, both sexually and emotionally. She brought him into her world the way she wanted him to see it.

Sharee had used her body, in so many ways, to intrigue, seduce, and trap the ex-homicide detective. The only thing that brought her down in the end was Cassaday's conscience on his dying day.

Further, Sharee's actions after her husband's death provided a possible motive for Bruce's murder other than Sharee's freedom. Money.

While Sharee had been loose with money during her marriage, she had gone over-the-top after her husband's death. She used Bruce's life insurance money to dramatically renovate her new inherited home within weeks of his death. She bought herself a new car and spent thousands of dollars on a plethora of items.

When Bruce died, Sharee inherited the family home she had grown so attached to as well as large sums of money both from Bruce's life insurance policy and also from the sale of his auto scrapyard business. Most significantly, though, Sharee had inherited her freedom without having to sacrifice her own and her children's secure, stable life.

Chapter 13

In December, 2000, Sharee went on trial for murder and conspiracy to commit murder.

Throughout the trial, Sharee continued to maintain that the instant messages were forged, as she was innocent of everything. She was simply the victim of an angry lover's broken heart.

The prosecutor's relied heavily on forensic science in their case against Sharee Miller—specifically, on the forensic computer analysis which proved the authenticity of Sharee and Cassaday's messages.

Sharee's trial was a short one. It did not take the prosecutors long to form their case, and the defense presented little-to-no evidence to support Sharee's claims that she was being framed by a dead man.

Sharee was found guilty on the charges of second-degree murder and conspiracy to commit first-degree murder. She was sentenced to life without the possibility of parole.

But this was not the end of Sharee's story.

Chapter 14

In 2009, Sharee Miller was released from prison after serving only nine years of a life without parole sentence. Her release was mandated by a U.S. District Judge who believed that the convicted killer had grounds for a new trial. This was because Jerry Cassaday's suicide note had been presented as damning evidence against Sharee in court despite the fact that Cassaday could not be cross-examined regarding the information in the letter.

Sharee spent a whole three years outside of bars. During this time, she kept a fairly low profile. She stayed in Flint with family, who she spent the most time with. She also spent the three years reconnecting with her sons—the children she spent most of her younger life fighting to support. Sharee's luck finally seemed to be turning in her favor.

But lady luck is fickle. In 2012, Sharee was ordered back to prison by the U.S. Supreme Court. The court disapproved of Sharee's release and mandated that the judge repeals her earlier decision to grant Sharee a new trial. The Supreme Court believed that there was enough additional evidence presented by the prosecutors, with no viable defense to counter it, that the outcome of the trial would have been the same had the suicide note not been presented at all.

Sharee's lawyers told the public that she was simply "disappointed" by her return to prison.

After returning to prison, Sharee and her lawyers quickly filed several appeals targeted at both the decision to return Sharee to court and her original guilty conviction, both of which were lost. Sharee was set to spend the rest of her life in prison for good this time.

That again seemed like the end of Sharee's story until late April 2016.

Seventeen years after manipulating Jerry Cassaday into killing her husband, Sharee Miller admitted her involvement in the crime for the first time through a letter addressed to a County Judge.

In this letter, Sharee claimed that she got caught up in the fantasy world she created with Cassaday. She like being the victim. It was more exciting to her than her real, stable life. However, she quickly found herself in too deep. She had created a monster and the only real way she saw of getting out was through the murder.

If Bruce were to die, neither he nor his family would ever have to discover what she was doing behind his back.

Sharee stated in her confessional letter that she did not enjoy watching her husband die. She wrote, "I had sixteen and a half hours to stop it. And I didn't. I knew it was going to happen and I allowed it. I allowed a man to kill another man based on my lies and manipulation."

She also used her letter as an opportunity to publicly recant the horrible image she had painted of her husband through her messages with Cassaday. She confirmed that Bruce was nothing but a wonderful husband. He had never laid a finger on her, and he always treated herself and her three children with the utmost kindness and respect. She regretted being the reason her children lost such a wonderful father figure—something she had always wanted for them.

While Sharee certainly believed that her confession would put an end to the long-standing controversy surrounding her case, the kind of controversy that inspired both a novel and lifetime movie about her crime, it actually perpetuated a new kind strand of controversy.

To many, especially to Bruce's loved ones, Sharee's confession letter seemed too crafted to be sincere. Sharee was the woman who had manipulated men to kill and die for her all through text. Now, she seemed to be trying to manipulate her way to an earlier release through the same medium.

Whether Sharee will claim another victim as a fool, this time a court judge, is yet to be seen.

JAMES & CYNTHIA

Natalie Morganis

James Marlow and Cynthia Coffman were a troubled couple who were convicted of murdering five people during a deadly rampage that spanned multiple states. The last two victims, 20-year old Corrina Novis and 19-year old Lynell Murray were kidnapped and found strangled and sodomized, and the murderous pair were found guilty of the crimes. Whereas both Marlow and Coffman received the death penalty for Novis' death, Marlow received a second death sentence for Murray's while Coffman was sentence to life without the possibility of parole in Murray's murder. Both defendants sought to shift the onus of blame to the other with Marlow claiming it was Coffman's idea to kill the girls while he only wanted to rob them and Coffman alleging that she was the victim of battered women's syndrome. Neither ploy was successful as the pair were convicted across the board for robbery, kidnapping, sodomy, and murder. Coffman has the distinction of being the first woman sentenced to death in California following the state's reinstatement of the death penalty in 1977.

Early Lives

James

James Gregory Marlow was born on 11 May 1956 in Ohio but raised in Kentucky; the son of a beautiful but amoral hillbilly woman named Doris who virtually ensured that her son would grow up completely dysfunctional. Throughout his childhood, Marlow witnessed abuse, neglect, drug use, and sex courtesy of his mother who often prostituted herself in front of him. She gave birth to another child, Veronica Koppers, in 1959 and would frequently leave her children alone or with neighbors. Marlow eventually went to live with his father, Arnold, who would beat him severely and lock him in cabinets and, subsequently, went back to his mother's house. Despite the abuse and her horrific behavior, Marlow loved his mother dearly. So much, in fact, that when he was 13 years old his mother shot him up with drugs and seduced him. During interviews Marlow openly admitted to having had sexual relations with his mother on several occasions and that he didn't know it was wrong. He loved his mother so much and thought it was normal. Experts assert that Marlow suffered from traumatic bonding in which a traumatic event—his mother's seduction—created a dysfunctional yet significant bond from which he could not escape.

By the time Marlow was 16 years old he was living alone in California and married his first of three wives. Thanks to his mother, Marlow developed a severely skewed view of women. When she died in a trailer fire he was completely distraught and "took on the sins of his parents" by turning to a life of crime and violence. In one incident when he was still a teenager, Marlow was talking to one of his cousin's girlfriend, Darlene Miller, who he—one day while driving her to a nearby convenience store—pulled over in front of an old, abandoned house and forced Miller into the house where he beat and hogtied her, and then locked her in a closet. Over a span of three days Marlow would repeatedly beat, rape, and sodomize Miller. She escaped and ran to a neighbor's house—a house that Marlow had recently burglarized. Police were called and Marlow was arrested and after a tearful pretrial interview wherein he tearfully detailed the issues with his mother, he was sent to a drug rehabilitation center in 1975 for seven months and, soon after his release in 1976 was rearrested for being under the influence. Marlow was eventually imprisoned for burglary, robbery, and drug charges and was ultimately sentenced to California's notorious Folsom Prison in 1980. It was here that Marlow—not unlike the majority of inmates—got heavily tattooed with one—a howling wolf on his right side—earning him the nickname of the Folsom Wolf.

Prior to meeting Coffman, Marlow had an extensive criminal record. On 5 November 1979 in Upland, California, Marlow and his friend Allen Smallwood, who were both heroin addicts, assaulted Jeffrey Johnson in his apartment, searched it for non-existent drugs, then took Johnson downstairs—by knifepoint—to the Liesches' apartment where they searched the second apartment for more non-existent drugs, tied up the residents—Lori and Kathy—with electrical cords, and stole some cash they had found.

The following day, Marlow entered an Upland, California, leather goods store owned by Joanne Gilligan who was helping a customer, said he had a gun in his pocket and ordered them to lie on the floor, and then robbed the register of cash and took two jackets.

At approximately 10:00 a.m. on 20 November that same year, Gertrude Smith and Wilson Lee were working at an Ontario, California, methadone clinic when Marlow and Smallwood entered brandishing a sawed-off shotgun and pistol, respectively, and demanded methadone which they were told was locked in a safe. Another employee opened the safe and the two left with methadone that had a street value of $10,000. When Marlow was finally arrested on 26 November he had a bottle of methadone in his jacket and had the shotgun wrapped in a shirt.

Cynthia

Cynthia Lynn Haskins was born on 19 January 1962 in St. Louis, Missouri. From the beginning her life was to be difficult. Born with a double hernia that precluded her mother from holding her, Cynthia never experienced the necessary mother-infant bonding so crucial for healthy adjustment. As a result, she suffered from a crucial lack of empathy and a driving propensity to seek affections elsewhere. Cynthia's father left when she was three years old and her mother—who had aspirations of becoming a singer—allegedly tried to give her and her brothers Robbie and Jeff away several times during their childhood; with Jeff eventually given up for adoption. Cynthia was frequently "farmed out" to relatives that made her become more rebellious, defiant, and reckless. By the time she was a sophomore in high school, Cynthia was already experimenting with marijuana and methamphetamine with her new friends.

Her mother remarried a successful businessman named Bill Maender with whom Cynthia did not get along. Truancy, rebelliousness, and ultimately not wanting to live by her stepfather's rules caused Cynthia to run away at age 17 to her boyfriend's, Ron Coffman, house. When Cynthia returned three months later, pregnant, abortion was not an option for her devout parents and she refused to give the baby up for adoption, so she was forced into a loveless marriage with Coffman. The marriage quickly deteriorated and Ron filed for divorce because of Cynthia's infidelities, drug use, and poor housekeeping while Cynthia accused him of physical and emotional abuse and infidelity. Cynthia then worked in a carburetor factory to take care of her son, Joshua. She ultimately abandoned Joshua after two years, leaving him with her ex-husband (allegedly intending to get him back after she got settled) although later, when she and Marlow were committing their heinous crimes she suggested that Marlow kill her ex-husband and ex-in-laws (who had legal custody of Joshua) so she could regain custody of her son. While on death row Coffman exchanges letters with her son who believes his mother to be in prison for drug-related charges. She has stated in interviews that she wants to be the one to tell him the truth someday.

There is much speculation that Coffman had antisocial personality disorder which is characterized by little regard for right and wrong or the feelings of others. Further, those with the chronic disorder tend to manipulate, antagonize, and treat others with a callous indifference, are very prone to violate the law, are easily angered, lie, behave impulsively and/or violently, and use and abuse drugs and alcohol—all without remorse or guilt. Coffman exhibited a number of these traits, many of which worsened once she began her relationship with Marlow.

In May 1984 Coffman left home with a girlfriend and journeyed west where she wound up in Page, Arizona, and moved in with her new boyfriend, Doug Huntley. The lovebirds moved to Barstow, California where Huntley had some friends. He secured employment in construction while she was a bartender and waitress and sold methamphetamines on the side. One evening they were involved in an altercation outside of a convenience store in which Coffman pulled a gun on several men who were hassling her boyfriend and this resulted in both Huntley and Coffman being arrested and jailed. While Coffman was released after a few days, Huntley became cellmates with Marlow. Huntley told Marlow all about Coffman which intrigued Marlow who, upon his release soon thereafter, showed up at Coffman's apartment. It was love at first sight as Coffman reminded Marlow of his mother and Marlow was every bit the bad boy to whom Coffman was attracted. Even after Huntley was released, Marlow, Coffman, and he remained friends until Huntley returned to prison in June of that year.

A Dangerous Partnership

Marlow and Coffman began their contentious, dysfunctional, and murderous relationship amidst drugs and violence; her former boyfriend Huntley all but forgotten. In June 1986 Marlow had Coffman drive him to Fontana, California, and to his cousin Debbie Schwab's house where he purchased methamphetamines. A few days later they went to Newberry Springs and stayed with some of Marlow's friends, Steve and Karen Schmitt. Marlow told Coffman that he was a hit man, a martial arts expert, and a White supremacist who had murdered African American while in prison. It was during this time that Coffman saw Marlow turn into "Wolf"—his angry, violent alter-ego. Coffman testified in court that Marlow would beat her and then apologize and things would be fine again for a while. This is classic cycle-of-violence behavior central to most domestic violence cases. At this point Marlow allegedly took Coffman's address book that had her mother's and son's addresses and refused to give it back to her; essentially holding it as a carrot just out of reach to get her to do what he wanted.

They traveled across the country visiting Marlow's relatives in Kentucky and Tennessee. He had told Marlow that his father had recently died and left him some land in Kentucky and that they could get her son and live as a family there. First, however, they needed a vehicle and Marlow allegedly pressured Coffman to steal her friend's red Nissan pickup truck that Marlow and friend Paul Donner painted black. Marlow and Coffman jumped in the truck, stole some license plates from an off road vehicle outside of Newberry Springs, California, and headed east.

In Woodland Park, Colorado, Marlow called Gene Kelly, a contractor who constructed microwave telephone relay towers and who Marlow had met when he was a temporary laborer for him a few years back, to see if he needed any help in Colorado at the time. (There is some discrepancy in the available literature with respect to this individual being named Gene Kelly or Elmer Lutz; however, the actual criminal case against the defendants state Kelly). Kelly told him that he didn't have any work at the time but that he would have some work in Atlanta, Georgia, in a few weeks. The couple went to Colorado Springs for a couple of days and then to St. Louis to see Coffman's grandmother. They arrived on 2 July and Coffman called her mother who was less than happy to hear from her. The couple continued their journey east.

In Pine Knot, Kentucky, Marlow called his cousin Donald "Lardo" Lyons and both he and Coffman stayed with him for several days. Marlow had expected a modest inheritance from his grandmother Lena Walls with whom Marlow and his sister Veronica were close when they were younger; however, by the time Marlow reached Kentucky there was nothing left for him. Needing money, Marlow agreed to meet with Lardo's friend Shannon "Killer" Compton and the trio discussed how a local man named Greg "Wildman" Hill was going to be testifying in court against a mutual acquaintance and that Hill should "be silenced." They arranged for Compton to give Lyons a sum of money of which Lyons would give $5,000 to Marlow to get rid of Hill.

The next day, 7 July 1986, Lyons gave Marlow a .22 caliber pistol and at 5:00 a.m. Marlow and Coffman got into their stolen black Nissan pickup and drove to Hill's house. For most of the day the two of them parked relatively close and surveilled his house, did drugs, and engaged in sex. Finally, Marlow ordered Coffman to take off her shirt and bra and to tie a bandana across her chest like a bikini top and to knock on Hill's door to elicit help for her "stalled" truck. Hill agreed and tucked his own pistol inside his jeans' waistband. At the truck, when Marlow came after Hill with his own gun, Hill drew his and after an ensuing struggle Hill's gun went off, mortally wounding him with a bullet to the head. Marlow wiped his fingerprints off Hill's gun and left it at the scene.

Lyons kept true to his word giving Marlow the $5,000 "fee" for his "hit." The next day Marlow gave the stolen Nissan to a relative and spent $3,000 on a Harley Davidson; something he wanted for a very long time. On 11 July 1986 Marlow and Coffman had a "biker" wedding atop a Marlow's new Harley. Witnesses alleged that Coffman's face was bruised and scratched from a recent beating Marlow have given her. Such violence was not an isolated incident. In fact, one time while Marlow was assaulting Coffman one of his acquaintances asked what he was doing and Marlow dislocated his arm. As a result, nobody else ever intervened when Marlow was in one of his rages against Coffman. She said that when Marlow turns into "Wolf" his voice becomes monotone and his eyes and facial expression changes—that he becomes a completely different and violent person.

Marlow ended up giving the Nissan to a friend and purchasing a 1970's Cadillac to continue their journey to Atlanta and a job with Kelly. Marlow did manage to work for four days before an incident wherein he, Coffman, and a group of coworkers went out for dinner but which turned into Marlow beating Coffman outside of the restaurant and inside the vehicle, seemingly because she assisted some men with a stuck ball at a pool table. Back at the hotel where they were staying, Marlow was not finished with Coffman. He asked her for her scissors and then queried, "Your hair or your eye?" Horrified, Coffman said her hair and Marlow cut it as short as he could with her small scissors. He then taunted her that he would pierce her eye as well before making her strip naked and forcing her to stand outside the hotel room for several minutes. He then let her back into the room where he forcibly sodomized her. The following morning Marlow found a check from Kelly that had been slid under the door for his four days of work. After a few more days of going on "pot hunts" and unsuccessfully attempting a burglary in July 1986 in Whitley County, Kentucky, the couple left and headed back to Arizona.

In Arizona, Marlow and Coffman burglarized her former boyfriend Doug Huntley's parents' house and stole their safe that contained ten silver dollars—which they kept—and some papers. They buried the safe in the dessert. The next stop was back in Newberry Springs, California, where the couple stole two rings from the Schmitts; one they pawned for cash and the other they traded for methamphetamines.

Returning to Fontana, California, in early October 1986, Marlow and Coffman stayed with his cousins, the Schwabs. During their visit Marlow tattooed "Property of Folsom Wolf" on Coffman's buttocks and the word "W-O-L-F" and some lightning bolts on her ring finger as a wedding band. They then spent some time with Marlow's friends Rita Robbeloth and her son Curtis, and then with his sister, her husband Paul Koppers, and his brother, Steve. During this time Coffman alleges that after asking for an equal share of the methamphetamine they had, Marlow became angry and beat her, threatened to kill her, forced her to consume pills he said were cyanide, extinguished a cigarette on her face, and stabbed her in the leg. The pair then went to stay with another of Marlow's friends, Richard Drinkhouse.

The Crimes

On 11 October 1986 they were linked to the death of 32-year old Sandra Neary of Costa Mesa, California who never returned from a quick trip to a local ATM machine to withdraw some money. Her car was found in a nearby parking lot and her body was later found on 24 October by some hikers near Corona, California. Their next victim was 35-year old Pamela Simmons. She was reported missing in Bullhead City, Arizona, on 28 October. Her abandoned car was found by the local police department and the theory was that she was also abducted while withdrawing money from an ATM.

Corinna Novis

On 7 November, 20-year old Corinna Novis vanished from a First Interstate Bank parking lot near a shopping mall in Redlands, California, in broad daylight. Alone, she was driving her white Honda CR-X and when she failed to make her manicure appointment at her friend Terry Davis' salon, and then failed to make a 7:00 p.m. pizza date with other friends, she was reported missing. That same day, Marlow and Coffman were at the Redlands Mall visiting his sister Koppers who worked at a restaurant and were supposed to pick her up from work; however, Marlow gave his sister back her keys, telling her that they already had a ride. Coffman, clad in a dress, and Marlow, in a suit and tie, probably seemed rather innocuous to Novis when they asked her for a ride. Earlier that day Marlow had told Coffman that they needed to "get a girl" but Coffman alleged that she did not know that Marlow intended to kill her.

At approximately 7:30 p.m., they took Novis to Marlow's friend Richard Drinkhouse's house who was home alone recovering from a motorcycle accident at the time. Coffman took their hostage into the bedroom after telling Drinkhouse they needed to use the bathroom. Marlow told Drinkhouse that Coffman was trying to get her ATM pin number so they could "rob" her bank account. Drinkhouse didn't appreciate their intrusion into his house to which Marlow assured Drinkhouse that that there wouldn't be any witnesses because how could Novis talk to anyone "if she's under a pile of rocks"? Soon thereafter, Marlow's sister Koppers showed up and she and Coffman left the house to go to a nearby 7-Eleven while Marlow cautioned Drinkhouse not to leave and then returned to the bedroom where Novis was. After Coffman returned, she went into the bedroom to change clothes and after what sounded like the shower running the three of them emerged from the bedroom—Novis' and Marlow's hair were wet (Coffman testified that she had nothing to do with "what went on in the shower"). Novis was handcuffed and had duct tape over her mouth. They left the house and Drinkhouse testified that he never saw Novis again.

The next day, Marlow and Coffman asked Drinkhouse if he wanted to buy an answering machine. Novis' employer Jean Cramer, went to check on her the morning of 10 November when she uncharacteristically failed to appear at work and didn't call. She noticed Novis' car was missing, her front door was ajar, and her bedroom was in disarray. There was no evidence of forced entry and Novis' typewriter and answering machine were missing. On 7 November Koppers sold Novis' answering machine to a friend in exchange for a half-gram of methamphetamine who sold it to someone else and the Redlands Police Department ultimately recovered it. The next day, Harold Brigham who owned the Sierra Jewelry and Loan in Fontana testified that Coffman pawned Novis' typewriter using the victim's identification.

Back at the Robbeloths' house Coffman said Marlow changed clothes and tried to access money from Novis' account at a local First Interstate Bank; however, the PIN number she gave them was incorrect. The following day they ransacked Novis' apartment, found her PIN number, stole her money, pawned the typewriter they stole, disposed of Novis' belongings and then returned to Drinkhouse's house. On 12 November Marlow found out that his sister was in police custody and he and Coffman drove to Big Bear to get rid of Novis' car. They checked into the Bavarian Lodge using a credit card from another victim, Lynell Murray. They abandoned Novis' car on a dirt road south of Santa's Village which was approximately a quarter mile off of Highway 18 in the area. Coffman's fingerprints were found on the license plate, hood, and ashtray while Marlow's prints were found on the hood. The two then proceeded to walk along Big Bear Boulevard clad only in bathing suits despite the chilly weather; the stolen clothes that they had been wearing were discarded along with the handcuffs used on Novis. Receipts for clothing purchased by Marlow and Coffman were found in the clothing's pockets. The .22 caliber pistol the couple owned was in Coffman's purse.

Novis' body was discovered on 15 November lying face down in a shallow grave at a Fontana vineyard. She had been strangled and sodomized.

Dr. Gregory Reiber performed Novis' autopsy on 17 November and conclude that time of death was between five and ten days prior. Evidence of marks on her neck, injuries to her neck muscles, and thyroid cartilage fracture suggested death by strangulation; however, the presence of dirt in her throat also suggested possible suffocation. There was also biological evidence of sodomy.

Lynell Murray

On 12 November, 19-year old psychology student and Prime Cleaners dry cleaning shop clerk Lynell Murray failed to keep a date with her boyfriend, Robert Whitecotton, in Orange County. After noticing that the cleaners looked as though it had been burglarized and ransacked and that Murray's car was parked in the parking lot out back he called the police.

Murray had no idea that the previous day Marlow and Coffman saw her leaving work and that Marlow had commented that she would be "a good one to rob." The following evening at approximately 6:00 p.m., shortly before Murray was to leave work, one Lynda Schafer entered the cleaners and dropped of some clothes with Murray. Schafer would later testify that she saw Coffman "passionately embracing a man", later identified as Marlow, in an alley behind the cleaners.

At 6:30 p.m. that evening Coffman approached Linda Whitlake who was leaving her gym and asked for a ride to her motel, claiming that her car wouldn't start. After Whitlake noticed Marlow in Novis' white car with its hood up she changed her mind about giving them a ride. Coffman said that her boyfriend had decided to call the auto club instead and Whitlake left.

At 7:13 p.m. Coffman checked into room 307 of the Huntington Beach Inn under the name Lynell Murray and used Murray's credit card. At 8:19 p.m. a Bank of America branch in Corona del Mar recorded a balance inquiry into Murray's account and a subsequent withdrawal of $80 occurred, shortly followed by a $60 withdrawal, which left a balance of $4.41. Later that evening Coffman checked into the Compri Hotel in Ontario, California, with Murray's credit card. At midnight Marlow and Coffman ate dinner at the Denny's restaurant across from the hotel, which they paid for with Murray's credit card.

Murray's body would be discovered the following day at approximately 3:00 p.m. in room 307 at the Huntington Beach Inn. Her head was in the bathtub in six inches of water with it and her face bound with strips of towel. She was gagged. Her right arm was secured to her waist with a towel. Her right leg was atop the toilet and her left leg was on the floor. Her ankles looked to have been bound with duct tape as residue was evident. Her bra, nylons, and one earring were missing and she looked to have been raped and urinated on. She had also suffered pre-mortem blunt force trauma to the head, torso injuries, two black eyes, and leg bruising which were consistent with being beaten. The cause of death was determined to be ligature strangulation.

Police finally turned their attention to Marlow and Coffman after finding Novis' driver's license and checkbook in a Taco Bell takeout bag near a dumpster in Laguna Niguel along with papers with both Marlow's and Coffman's names on them. Marlow had attempted to dispose of this damning evidence but missed the dumpster. A statewide alert was issued for both Marlow and Coffman.

Arrest

On 14 November, police were dispatched to a Big Bear, California, mountain lodge after being alerted that Murray's credit card was being used to purchase clothes at a local sporting goods store. The owner of the lodge identified Marlow and Coffman as his latest guests. After finding the lodge empty, the 100-man posse discovered the suspects walking along a mountain road at approximately 3:00 p.m. They surrendered without incident, clad in clothing they had stolen from the dry cleaning shop where Murray had worked. A few hours later Coffman led police to Novis' body. One of the victim's earrings, a .22 caliber pistol and ammunition, credit card receipts with Murray's forged signature, and a Prime Cleaners paper bag with coins were found in Coffman's purse.

The Trial

Nearly three years later Marlow and Coffman would stand trial which commenced on 18 July 1989 in San Bernardino County. At several points throughout the proceedings motions for severance filed by both defendants were denied.

Among the overwhelming evidence were both defendants' fingerprints in Novis' car and that, as previously mentioned, Coffman was linked to the Fontana pawn shop where Novis' typewriter was pawned. In room 307 of the Huntington Beach Inn where Lynell Murray's body was found, a footprint on a bathmat by her body was consistent with Marlow's boots. The aforementioned Taco Bell bag with Novis' license and checkbook and documentation with Coffman's and Marlow's names was recovered. Credit card activity demonstrated where and when the defendants had used Murray's credit card. Additionally, the discarded suit jacket that Marlow had worn when they abducted Novis was found at the Bavarian Lodge and contained identification bearing Marlow's name, various single earrings presumed to be trophies from the murders, a blue ladies wallet, and the handcuffs used on Novis. Novis' vehicle was found near Santa's Village with license plates stolen from a vehicle that was at the Huntington Beach Inn and in a nearby trash can a maintenance worker found a pillowcase containing Murray's bra and laundry receipts from the cleaners where Murray had worked.

Coffman took the stand in her own behalf, painting Marlow to be an abusive man who was violent toward her and threatened both her and her son. She alleged that any violence directed toward the victims were perpetrated by Marlow. With respect to Novis, Coffman testified that on the night of Novis' death, she had dropped Novis and Marlow off at the vineyard and was told to go purchase methamphetamines. Coffman alleges that she drove a short distance, stopped and smoked a cigarette, and then returned to "the sound of digging." Marlow returned to the vehicle alone, threw some items in the back of the car, and then started to beat her for driving away.

Coffman's attorney presented numerous witnesses who corroborated Coffman's allegations of Marlow's violence including Katherine Davis, one of Marlow's ex-wives, and her mother Marlene Boggs; Coffman's former employers in Arizona; Coffman's mother Carol Maender; and clinical psychologist Craig Rath who claimed that Coffman's relationship with Marlow was "precipitated by impaired bonding in her early life", that she was not malingering, and that she did not suffer from antisocial personality disorder.

In Marlow's defense, his sister Veronica Koppers testified about the abuse and neglect the two suffered at the hands of their mother and her father Wendell Hill; about how her father shot her mother and her mother stabbed her father seven times which prompted Doris to move to California in 1963; about visiting her mother at the Sybil Brand Institute for Women and the Frontera State Prison; about how Doris introduced her daughter to drugs much like she did with Marlow and taught her how to burglarize houses; and about the myriad drinking and drug parties hosted at their house. Several witnesses at the trial testified that Doris rarely even mentioned that she had children and paid them little attention when they were together. Despite Marlow claiming responsibility for the murder in Kentucky as well as Novis' and Murray's in California he tried to shift the majority of blame onto Coffman much as she attempted to do to him.

Throughout the trial, Coffman's legal team tried to utilize the "Patty Hearst" defense that she was brainwashed, starved, and the victim of battered women's syndrome who was subjected to frequent physical, emotional, and mental abuse. Once, she claimed, Marlow beat her with a motorcycle clutch plate bruising her face and another time kicked her with his steel-toed boots. She stated that she feared for both her life and that of her then-six-year old son. Coffman's side even presented an expert on battered women's syndrome; however, the jury apparently rejected such claims.

Other testimony suggested that Coffman was the true ringleader and cold, calculated murderess, being far more intelligent than Marlow who would do anything to keep her. At one point, prosecutor Robert Gannon asked Coffman whether her relationship with Marlow was more important than the lives of Corinna Novis and Lynell Murray to which she replied, "Yes."

Sentencing

Both defendants were convicted of the kidnapping, robbery, kidnapping for robbery, residential burglary, forcible sodomy, and murder of Novis and subsequently sentenced to death on 30 August 1989. Coffman became the first women sentenced to death in California since the state reinstated capital punishment in 1977; however, California's reputation as an overly liberal state makes it unlikely that Coffman will ever be put to death.

On 8 March 1992 Marlow received a second death sentence for Murray's murder while Coffman received a life without the possibility of parole sentence added to her death sentence, the former rather moot.

On 19 August 2004 the California Supreme Court unanimously upheld both Marlow's and Coffman's death sentences.

Post-conviction

There continues to be speculation as to whether Coffman controlled or was controlled by Marlow. In fact, while on Death Row, Marlow wrote *I Wish You Were Never Born*, a novel detailing Coffman's and his murderous spree (proceeds of the sale of his book are donated to help abused children). He asserts that their story in the popular media—including an episode of *Wicked Attractions*—was sensationalized and he wanted the truth to be known.

PSYCHO GIRL : THE TRUE STORY OF CATHERINE BIRNIE

48

JENA DICKENS

Catherine Margaret Harrison was born on May 23rd, 1951. Her partner, David John Birnie, was born on February 16th, 1951 and died on October 7th, 2015 by way of suicide. The duo was famously known throughout Australia as: The Killer Couple. They were from Perth, Australia and were found to have murdered four women ranging in age from 15 to 31 years old, over a span of about five weeks. Their fifth victim managed to escape through the bedroom window, while Catherine was distracted by a knock at the front door. The woman immediately ran and found help. The press referred to the heinous murders as the Moorhouse Murders. The victims were taken to Catherine and David's home located at 3 Moorhouse Street in Willagee, in Western Australia, a suburb of Perth.

Catherine was only two years old when her mother died in childbirth while giving birth to Catherine's younger brother. Her brother also died, two days later. Catherine's father, Harold, couldn't manage raising Catherine on his own at that time so she went to live with her maternal grandparents. When she was ten years old, Harold petitioned the court to receive custody of Catherine again, and he won. There always seemed to be a battle. Catherine's father didn't want her, but then wanted her, always back and forth. After Catherine was convicted of four counts of murder, it caused her father to suffer a nervous breakdown.

When Catherine was twelve years old she met a boy named David Birnie and they began dating two years later when they became teenagers. Both Catherine and David came from dysfunctional families. Their home life was chaotic and messy, literally as well as figuratively. David's mother was an alcoholic and his father was away at work the majority of the time. His father died in 1986 after battling a long illness. The house, as well as his mother, were messy and unkempt. She left her older children in charge of taking care of their younger siblings. She refused to do anything when it concerned the children and their welfare. Allegedly, David's mother would leave the refrigerator door open so that the children could eat throughout the day. David was the oldest of five children. David's school friends, as well as the local priest, deemed the family dysfunctional. The parents never prepared meals for their children, the house was always a mess, and the Priest, before marrying David's parents, said that he felt that their marriage would never lead to anything good. Little did he know how accurate his assumptions would be.

Catherine and David met through mutual friends shortly after David's family moved to the same Perth neighborhood as Catherine and her father. Catherine's father felt that David was trouble and a bad influence. Catherine had begun getting into a lot of trouble with the local police ever since the two of them met. Harold begged and pleaded with Catherine to stay away from David and stay out of trouble. Of course, this just brought the two closer. Whenever two kids are told not to do something, they go out of their way to blatantly disobey.

Even in adolescence David began exhibiting violent and perverse behavior. When David turned fifteen he dropped out of school and began working as jockey apprentice for Eric Parnham at the Ascot Race Course. While there, David would hurt the horses and also began his perverse career as an exhibitionist. David committed his first rape shortly after. By this point he had spent time in and out of jail for several charges ranging from misdemeanors to felonies. He built up a reputation around town as a sex and pornography addict.

Catherine was an accessory to a lot of crimes because of her involvement with David. They built up an extensive history of numerous charges including: breaking and entering, trespassing, unlawfully driving a motor vehicle, and theft. Catherine took the time, while in jail, to decide it was time to get away from David and start over. David had to serve a long jail sentence, while Catherine got off with probation. With the help of her parole officer, she found a job as a housekeeper working for the McLaughlin family. She ended up marrying the families' oldest son, Donald McLaughlin, on her twenty first birthday. They went on to have seven children. One of her children, however, was killed in a car accident while he was only an infant, leaving her with six of her children to take care of. Catherine was never really interested in motherhood though, and wasn't proud of her children and her family like another mother might be. She wasn't concerned about the children or keeping up with the house. Catherine was never truly happy. Her thoughts kept going back to her childhood love, David Birnie. The family that she had left never saw Catherine as a violent or evil person. Not unless she was around David.

Catherine finally reconnected with David Birnie after a thirteen year separation, four weeks after she gave birth to their seventh child. David had escaped from prison and the two of them had begun seeing each other. Catherine left her family and everything behind when David popped back into her life. They finally moved in together and Catherine had her last name changed to Birnie, although the couple never formally or legally got married. They moved into a white brick, two bedroom bungalow on Moorhouse Street. The house was unkempt, the property looked untended, and the house needed a fresh coat of paint. Catherine was completely dependent on David, emotionally and physically. Catherine was easily controlled and manipulated by David, and she would do anything and everything to make him happy. She never wanted to disappoint him. David had an insatiable sexual appetite and was said to have sex up to six times a day. He also accrued an extensive pornography collection and his brother claimed he always had someone. He always had a woman around. David's brother, James, had ended up staying with Catherine and David for a short while. James had just recently been released from prison after serving time for his own sex related offenses. He stayed with the couple for about six months. His brother went on to describe the numbing spray that David would spray on his penis before he had sex with all of the different women.

David and Catherine had exhausted all of their options sexually and began looking for new ways to pleasure themselves. They had spoken about abduction and rape, but had not realized that it would be just a few short weeks before they turned their fantasies into a heinous and perverted reality. Being as emotionally dependent on David as she was, it was easy for David to talk her into his abduction and rape plans. Catherine could never tell him no. She felt that she couldn't survive without him and would do anything to keep him. Catherine was completely codependent and David always seemed to be in control. She wanted David to have all the pleasure and excitement that he wanted but knew that they had exhausted all efforts between just the two of them.

The abductions, rapes, and brutal murders began on October 6th, 1986. The couple didn't really care who their victims were, as long as they were female and alone. Twenty two year old Mary Neilson arrived at the Moorhouse Street residence to inquire about some tires that David had for sale. Mary was a student at the University of Western Australia where she was pursuing her degree in Psychology. Once inside the house, David took Mary by knife point and chained her to their bed and gagged her. Catherine stood in the room and watched as David raped the girl repeatedly. After the rape, the couple took Mary to Gleneagles National Park. David raped her one more time and then strangled her with a nylon cord and stabbed her through the heart. The couple then buried Mary in a shallow grave. Catherine looked on while David committed these violent acts, however, she did not yet participate.

The second murder took place on October 20th. The victim was fifteen year old, Susannah Candy. Susannah was a high school student attending Hollywood High School. She lived with her parents and had two brothers and one sister. Catherine and David Birnie had been driving around for several hours that night in search of their next victim. The couple finally found a girl walking along Stirling Highway, by herself, trying to hitch a ride. As soon as she got into David's car she had a knife to her throat and she was taken to the Birnies' home. While at the home, she was forced to write letters to her family explaining that she decided to run away. David repeatedly raped Susannah while she lay bound and gagged. Catherine had gotten into the bed with them and tried to strangle her with the nylon cord, but Susannah began fighting back. They forced sleeping pills down her throat, and once she passed out they successfully strangled her with the cord. The couple took Susannah to the State Park and buried her in a shallow grave, like their previous victims. This was the first time that Catherine took part in the murder. Catherine never showed any form of remorse over what she had done. When later asked why she contributed she said, "I wanted to see how strong I was within my inner self. I didn't feel a thing. It was like I expected. I was prepared to follow him to the end of the earth and do anything to see that his desires were satisfied. She was a female. Females hurt and destroy males."

On November 1st, the Killer Couple comes across their third victim, Noelene Patterson. Noelene was on her way home from work when her car ran out of gas. Noelene was a bar manager and had been working at Nedland's Golf Club that day. She was standing beside her car when David pulled up to her and offered his help. The thirty one year old got into David's car and was immediately met with a knife at her throat. She was taken to Moorhouse Street where she was bound and gagged, while being raped repeatedly. The original plan, like the others, was to kill the girl that same night. David had seemed to develop feelings for Noelene however. Catherine noticed the fondness that David had for the woman and became extremely jealous and increasingly upset. Noelene represented the type of person that Catherine could only wish to be and she absolutely despised her because of this. Catherine gave David an ultimatum at this point. She put the knife to her own chest and said, 'you either kill her tonight, or I will kill myself.' It was on the third night, after being given the ultimatum, that David gave Noelene several sleeping pills and then strangled her. She was then taken to the park and buried beside the other victims. Catherine admitted to taking pleasure in throwing sand in the victims face as David coldly buried her with no remorse.

Catherine and David's fourth victim, Denise Brown, suffered the same fate as the previous women who had the unfortunate experience of crossing paths with the Killer Couple. Denise Brown was twenty one years old, and was taken on November 5, 1986 while waiting at a bus stop. She was gagged and raped repeatedly before being put into the car and taken to Pine Plantation, where she was raped again while David waited for a blanket of darkness to fall. After it got dark he took her out and raped her again, while stabbing her in the neck. As David began burying her, thinking she was dead, Denise surprised the couple by sitting straight up in her grave. David struck her in the head twice with an axe as Catherine looked on in shock and amazement. David has said that he learned bodies would decompose at a faster rate if you stabbed them.

Detective Sergeant Paul Ferguson was the first to realize that he could be dealing with a serial killer, after the fourth woman was reported missing. Years later he recalled his experience while working on the case. He recalls how this case still haunts him and when asked why replied, "Because it was the most interesting and horrific I've had in my career," and "I have things tucked away back here that I pray to God I never pull out of the drawer." All of the missing women had come from relatively good homes and they never got into any real trouble. Their families found the phone calls and letters they received very suspicious.

The couples' fifth and final victim was seventeen year old Kate Moir. She was on her way home, after a night out with her friends, when she was abducted by the couple. The date of this final abduction was November 10th, 1986. Kate was the only one of their victims that was able to escape and run and find help. David had left the house for work that day. Catherine was home with Kate. She forced her to call her parents and tell them that she would be staying at a friend's house. When Catherine heard a knock at the door, she left Kate alone, untied, and went to see who was there. Kate took the opportunity to escape through the open window and ran half naked to the nearest store. She ran in crying and pleading for help. Kate was taken to the Palmyra police station and questioned. She was able to give the police a full description of Catherine and David, as well as inform the police of the couples' address. After their arrest, Catherine admitted to knowing Kate, but the couple said that the sexual acts were consensual and she was a willing participant. The police performed a search of the Birnie's home and found Kate's bag, as well as a pack of cigarettes that Kate had managed to hide in the ceiling in order to prove that she was there. After hours of questioning, Catherine and David finally admitted to the rape and murders of the four women and agreed to show the police where they had buried them. Three of the victims had been buried in Gleneagle State Forest and one on the Pine Plantation. The couple showed no emotion, whatsoever, as the police dug up the graves. David was the one who showed the police the locations of the women, except for one. Catherine insisted that she be the one to show them where Noelene was buried. She showed no regret, only anger. She spat on Noelene's grave and made her strong feelings of hate toward her very vocal to the detective. She explained to the police, in great detail, how much she despised Noelene Patterson. As they were leaving, David turned to Detective Katich and said chillingly, "What a pointless loss of young life." They showed absolutely no remorse for what they had done. This statement stuck with the detectives for years to follow. They couldn't believe how little the couple seemed to care or regret what they had been done. In some ways, however, they thought Catherine was relieved that it was finally over.

Catherine admitted to not caring about participating in the rapes and murders of the women, until they got to Denise Brown. "I think I must have come to a decision that sooner or later there had to be an end to the rampage. I had reached the stage when I didn't know what to do. I suppose I came to a decision that I was prepared to give her a chance." The brutal manner in which Denise was murdered seemed to hit Catherine hard. She witnessed David not only stab her repeatedly but strike her in the head with the axe. "Deep and dark in the back of my mind was yet another fear. I had a great fear that I would have to look at another killing like that of Denise Brown, the girl he murdered with the axe."

In response to Kate Moir's escape, due to Catherine's carelessness with her victim, she said, "I knew that it was a foregone conclusion that David would kill her, and probably do it that night. I was just fed up with the killings.

I thought if something did not happen soon it would simply go on and on and never end."

Kate Moir survived the abduction and attacks of Australia's most infamous serial killers. Instead of remaining a victim, she chose to be a survivor. She also sought to seek reform for the way her government handled cases like hers.

"I want to see no parole for wilful murder. I want a reintroduction of wilful murder as a charge. I want truth in sentencing. I want no parole for sex offenders and child sex offenders. We have been softening our justice system for years."

Kate Moir is a married woman and mother of three children. She constantly fights for the changes and justice she deserves. The following are quotes that were made by Kate, again concerning Catherine's parole and the possibility of her release.

"I want the legacy that I leave to be that of a survivor and a hero, not a victim. But enough is enough."

"I want the Attorney General to change the law and stop reviewing Catherine Birnie's parole. She does not apply for it herself, it is automatically reviewed and every time it happens, it causes me incredible pain."

"Every time I hear that her parole is being reviewed, I relive the nightmare. It causes significant trauma because I relive it and it feels like it happened yesterday. My name was always protected because I was a minor at the time I was captured, but due to the internet, if anybody googles my name it is everywhere and linked to the Birnie killings."

The couple appeared in court on November 12th, 1986. This was just two days after their fifth victim had escaped and they were arrested. The court proceedings took place at Fremantle Magistrates Court. They both refused any kind of representation, no plea was entered, bail was refused, and they were remanded into custody. Catherine allegedly took photos and the couple also recorded video of their criminal acts. At trial, the police were in possession of the video evidence. On February 10, 1987 a crowd gathered outside of the courthouse. When they saw the couple being ushered in for trial they screamed and chanted, "Hang the Bastards!" The community was outraged over the news of the serial killings that took place and wanted David and Catherine to receive the maximum sentence. They even wanted to reinstate the death penalty for David and Catherine Birnie.

Bill Power, the court reporter, spoke about the proceedings and the manners in which the couple acted while in court. He said that it would be something that would always stick with him, he would never forget.

"There was nothing distinctive about David and Catherine when they first appeared in court to face multiple murder charges in the serial killings which brought an end to the mystery of young women going missing off Perth streets."

"They were a rather nondescript, ordinary looking couple you might find running a petrol station in a country town. David was a weedy little man and Catherine his drab, slightly buxom wife with a very sour face. Both were accompanied by male police officers."

"If you have ever witnessed a wild cat go off, then try and imagine some hellcat in the confined spaces of a narrow staircase. Catherine Birnie fought against the guarding police officers and refused to allow any of them to touch her as she screamed and spat her words at them until she reached the dock and spotted her beloved, David. Only then did she calm down."

It had also been said previously, by some people in the community that the couple never looked like the type that could commit such violent acts. They looked like normal and ordinary people. But the secret horrors of what occurred in their home on Moorhouse Street would paint a very different image of the couple.

Trial Judge Justice Wallace said in trial, "Each of these horrible crimes were premeditated, planned, and carried out cruelly and relentlessly over a comparatively short period."

Right before Judge Wallace sentenced Catherine, he delivered the following message to her. He explained that he did not believe that even though she pled guilty, that she was truly sorry for what she had done. She had pled guilty and avoided a long trial, and spared the victims' families from having to relive over and over what happened to their loved ones, but she showed no remorse, no emotion, no sympathy

for the crimes she had committed with David
Birnie.

*"You willingly joined in the selection of your
unfortunate victims, carried them off at
knifepoint, and held them in captivity for the sole
purpose of the sexual gratification of your partner
in crime and then murdered them, lest you be
identified, and then finally mutilated them. You
personally extinguished the life of two of your
victims and certainly participated in the death of
the third. The only appropriate punishment is the
sentence I intend to impose, strict life security in
prison."*

Remember, Catherine was completely
devoted, obsessed, and brainwashed when it
came to David. She would do anything and
everything for him to make sure he was happy.
This is the driving factor that David used to
manipulate and control her. He needed an
accomplice and she was more than willing, and
he knew it. Catherine and David received four

separate life sentences for the abduction, torture, rape, and murder of Mary Neilson, Susannah Candy, Noelene Patterson, and Denise Brown. Under sentencing laws, their case was brought up every three years automatically for parole. Kate began a crusade to ensure that the couple remained in prison. She grew a social media presence and page entitled, We Support Kate, as well as worked with the Empowerment Foundation in an attempt to build an online reform petition. Kate also received support from Catherine's son, Peter. He chose not to release his surname to the public, due to the physical and emotional abuse he has been forced to face in relation to his mother's crimes. He had suffered personal and professional ruin, as soon as people learned about his family history. He had been turned down for jobs, lost jobs he had, and even lost his fiancé because of his family background. Peter was only five years old when his mother was arrested. He saw his mother on television because of it shortly after her arrest. When speaking out on the abuse he faced, he recalled horrible stories of what happened to him, and his siblings, while growing up. He also stated that the mandatory parole hearings, every three years, prevented him from getting on with his life. Having to hear about his mother and relive the violence his mother was responsible for every few years, was an interruption to his life, and it made it harder to maintain a sense of normalcy within his career life and personal life. In an interview with the West Australian, Peter stated, "I want the parole board to hear I don't want her out. I don't want to see her out." He also said, "I have had baseball bats to the head, I have been jumped on and kicked at. I have been knocked out."

After pleading guilty and receiving their sentences, David was initially sent to maximum security Fremantle Prison, he was eventually moved into solitary confinement. He did not get along with the other prisoners and was constantly getting into fights. The inmates frequently and violently attacked David. A day before he was due in trial for the charge of rape of an inmate, David hung himself in his jail cell. His suicide occurred in 2009 at Casuarina Prison. Catherine's request to attend David's funeral was refused.

Catherine was sent to Bandyup Women's prison where she was eventually employed as the head librarian. While in prison, the couple exchanged over 2600 letters, but were denied any other form of contact. Catherine's mandatory parole hearings were finally revoked in 2009, and her papers were subsequently marked: 'never to be released.'

While many people are against Catherine Birnie ever getting parole, one man stands against this argument. Perth QC Tom Percy disagrees with the opinion of people that had been saying that some people just don't deserve a second chance. The following quotes by Percy outline his argument of Catherine not remaining in prison and the likelihood of her harming the community, as well as his stance of being in favor of Catherine's parole.

"She should not be kept in prison to satisfy society's thirst for revenge."

"She has been there thirty odd years and you would think it might be time for us to say she has done her time. She has done her statutory minimum prescribed by the court, which was in possession of all of the facts."

"I am not sure she could really be a threat to anyone anymore, and all my information from Bandyup Womens' Prison is that she is a little old granny that goes about her work in the library like a church mouse."

"This case just so happened to be one that caught the public attention, even though she was not the prime mover in it. David is now dead."

"What's the point of keeping her in there? Sadly, it looks like she will never get parole, but I think she probably deserves it."

Despite his argument and fight to get Catherine released from prison, she still remains behind bars. She has not requested any new parole hearings, herself, as of yet. Some people in the community had gone as far as to say that if she were to be released, then maybe Percy should allow her to live with him in his residence.

It was now January of 1987. A letter written by Catherine Birnie, while in prison, eventually surfaced. It was a letter she had written to her six children in an attempt to explain some of her actions that led to her being placed in prison and why she left them in the first place. The letter reads as followed:

"Dear kids, Hi! Mum here...the reason I changed my name to Birnie was so that you kids wouldn't be hurt by the newspapers and television people. I am not proud of what has been said about me, but I have to live with that and the memories. As to why this happened, I can only hope that the doctors can help me to find out.....I never stopped loving any of you kids. Maybe I was wrong about leaving you but I thought you would be safer with your father."

Catherine's husband, Donald, claimed that he had still wanted her back. This was after trial and after he heard of the horrific acts she had committed with David. He stated, 'you can't stop loving someone after fifteen years of marriage.' Donald's mother stood firmly beside her son, saying that Catherine had been good and non-violent, until David cast his spell over her. Catherine's nephew, Leonard Nock, stood beside his aunt claiming, "All Aunt Cathy wanted was someone to lean on. She never had a mother. She is a very caring person. She and I are very close. I used to call her my mum. She was never the violent type, she never used to hit the kids. It is not the Cathy we used to know and love." In Catherine's letter she also persuaded the children to tell their father to divorce her. She said their father needed to move on and this was the way it needed to be done. She didn't hold out any hope for her eventual release and didn't want Donald to wait for her, because it was never going to happen. She also asked the children to get permission from Donald to write back to her, and maybe even one day go and visit her. The family put the entirety of the blame on David. They refused to admit to or believe that Catherine had anything to do with the violence. During their prison visits, the family also failed to even ask Catherine the question regarding her guilt or innocence. They didn't want to hear the answer, therefore, they never even asked the question.

Catherine Bernie was up for parole in 2013 and again in 2016. She was denied both years. She is once again up for review sometime in 2019. "Now barring any reason to keep her in, and revenge I don't consider enough of a reason. She should be released."-Percy

Despite Percy's statements, Catherine Birnie remains in prison to this very day, with little to no chance of parole. People, even to this day, wonder if the abductions, the perverse rape, and heinous murders would have continued long past the few weeks they had gotten away with it. If they had never been caught, would they have continued? Finally, were there other victims that they never confessed to? Other gravesites that have yet to be located? It is too late for David Birnie to tell anyone, but Catherine still has the chance to admit to any other wrongdoing she had done before her permanent home in prison forced her to keep distance between herself and her lover. I guess we will never know.

"I honestly believe that woman has never given those victims one ounce of consideration, both the dead victims and the families of the victims...They [David and Catherine Birnie] were parasites who lived off of each other. The most evil people I have ever, ever come across."-Detective Paul Ferguson.

BABY KILLER

The True Story of Amelia Dyer

Chrissy Eubank

Amelia Dyer, considered one of the most prolific serial killers in history, was born around 1837 in Victorian Britain. Her picture on the front cover easily betrays the evil that resided within her heart. Her reign of terror lasted over twenty years, as she is projected to have killed as many as 400 children before finally being caught

She embarked on a thirty year career of killing with eyewitnesses seeing at least six babies entering her house a day. The count of 400 dead is a conservative estimate.

EARLY LIFE

Amelia was the youngest of five children born into the tiny town of Pyle Marsh. She had three older brothers, Thomas, James, and William along with an older sister named Ann. Her father was a shoemaker named Samuel Hobley and her mother was named Sarah Weymouth.

But he didn't come from an impoverished family like so many others during the Victorian Era.

"For the time, she had a pretty good start," said author Allison Rattle. "Her father had a pretty good trade and paid for her to go to church and school which at the time only a quarter of the children her age actually got an education so she was privileged in that respect."

She found entertainment in reading and used to write poetry herself. Amelia's mother Sarah, however, became mentally ill after suffering from typhus fever. Amelia had to suffer through watching her mother's seizures and outbursts, providing care for her until she died in 1848.

"She witnessed her mother basically losing her mind," said Rattle. "And dying a slow, horrific death. I guess being a young girl she may have been called upon to nurse her mother slightly or at least wait upon her."

Psychologists have posited that it was going through this trauma of watching her mother lose her mind, that caused Amelia's own emotional wiring to run askew.

"Amelia would later claim that her mother died as a result of hereditary insanity," said author Allison Vale. "I think though that this isn't true but it's really easy to understand how she could have remembered it that way."

"It was certain to have a massive impact on her and she may have learned a few things about what kind of symptoms might be shown by someone whose losing their mind."

Amelia was sent to live with her aunt in nearby Bristol after her mother's death. She started an apprenticeship with a corset maker and worked there until her father died in 1859. The oldest brother, Thomas, took control of the family shoe business. Two years later, some type of estrangement occurred with her brothers, specifically James and Amelia doesn't appear to have further ties with her family.

In 1861, Amelia moved to Trinity Street, Bristol. She married George Thomas, who at 59 years old was 35 years Amelia's senior. The two lied about their ages on their marriage certificate with George claiming he was 48 years old and Amelia claiming she was 30.

A CAREER IN "HEALTH CARE"

Amelia began training as a nurse after she got married.

"Amelia turned to one of the most arduous professions she could have turned to," Vale said. "Nursing was just starting to change. It was post-Crimean war. Nursing was starting to have a much better profile as a result of Florence Nightingale. But it was still a thankless profession."

"It wasn't a caring profession like it is present day," agreed psychologist Laura Richards. "They train you psychologically to be a lot more robust around dealing with people. So she became quite hardy and emotionless from having been trained through the nursing regime."

Amelia became pregnant at the age of twenty-six before she met a woman named Ellen Dane who came to boarder at her house. Dane was a midwife who told her of a lucrative and shady way to earn money. Amelia would use her own home as a front to provide housing for women who had gotten pregnant out of wedlock. They would them give the babies away for adoption or kill them through malnutrition.

They called it baby farming.

"Amelia could see it was a very easy way to make money," Rattle said. "Although with risks involved obviously although Amelia did have training as a mid-wife as well through her nursing experience so it was certainly something she knew she was capable of doing. That was the beginning of a massive change in Amelia's life."

Dane moved her base of operations to the USA while Amelia took her "business plan" to heart. During this time, unmarried mothers did not have access to any kind of subsidy as the 1834 Poor Law Amendment Act did not oblige the fathers of illegitimate children to pay for their upbringing. These laws, coupled with the stigmatization of single mothers, forced the practice of baby farming.

Amelia discussed business strategies with Dane. She knew the best bet was to insist on being paid upfront with a one-time fee. She refused any type of money for continuous care as she knew that would mean the mother would return to visit.

"The one off premiums were certainly not enough to sustain a child's life for long financially," Vale said. "And the only way that it would be profitable for a baby farmer was to subject a child to persist underfeeding that would at some point bring about the infant's death."

"Abortion was not an option," Judith Knelman said. "So the simplest thing to do was hide, have the baby and get rid of it. Pay somebody to take care of it or pay somebody to get rid of it."

The babies were subsequently left on the premises and seen as "nurse children."

"Illegitimacy was seen as hugely immoral," said author Allison Rattle. "Even orphanages would only accept orphans from families where the parents were married and the father had died. They wouldn't accept a child who was born out of wedlock."

"Dickens did a really good job of describing social conditions in the 1850 and 60s," Knelman added. "Certainly there were a lot of poor people. There were a lot of neglected and abandoned children."

"There was no work," said Alan McCormick of Scotland Yard. "There was no social services. There was no welfare. One in every twelve women was a prostitute. A child being born in normal circumstances only had a fifty percent chance of reaching the age of five. So that's how bad it was."

BABY FARMING

"Baby farming was a business carried out throughout the country," said historian Ken Wells. "If a mother was unable to look after their child, there was an option of sending them out to a baby farmer, also known as fostering, with the understanding that they could visit the child whenever they wanted to."

On the surface they were providing a service to a growing need. They took an unwanted child and gave them to a foster parent. Only those foster parents and caregivers didn't always have the best interests of the infant at heart.

"MOTHER'S FRIEND"

The majority of these "caregivers" resorted to starving out the babies. They sedated crying babies with alcohol or drugs usually using Godfrey's Cordial, also known as 'Mother's Friend'. This syrup was one of the most popular medicines given to infants and children in both the United States and England in the latter years of the 18th and early 19th centuries. The syrup was used as a panacea to everything from colic to jaundice to excessive crying to diarrhea. 'Mother's Friend' was harmful despite its harmless sounding name as it contained one grain of opium for every two ounces. Many infants were poisoned from this syrup which was administered in secret by nurses who wanted to keep babies under their care in a deep state of sleep and thus more manageable.

"A hungry child, a noisy child, is a difficult child to raise," author Allison Vale said. "And something that was chillingly referred to colloquially as 'the Quietness' was an over the counter anti-colic cordial and it did contain liquid opium which was laudanum and in some cases brandy."

"People gave babies laudanum when they were supposed to be giving them food," Klansman said. "Because it dulled the need, or dulled the awareness of the baby that it was hungry. Of course it didn't nourish the baby so eventually a baby that was given that and not given enough food would die."

The babies would die from severe malnutrition but the coroner would record the death as "debility from birth", "lack of breast milk" or "starvation."

There were those guilt-ridden mothers who returned to the baby-farming homes to check on their children but would find their efforts blocked. Most would be too scared or embarrassed to inform the police of any wrongdoing. The police themselves had numerous problems tracking any children that were deemed missing.

"Dead infants," Vale said. "Or abandoned infants were as commonplace in British cities as roadkill today. Babies were found parceled up in railroad stations, under railroad arches."

"It was desperation," McCormick added. "For the vast majority of these ladies."

TO A MANNER BORN

With Dane's departure to the States, Amelia set her sights on taking her place in the baby-farming business. She had just given birth to her own daughter, Ellen, but in 1869 her husband George died.

A widow at age 32 with a baby, Amelia needed a new source of income...

She began taking in pregnant women as she placed ads to nurse and adopt the babies. In return, she required a large one-time fee and clothing for the child. She began meeting with expectant young women, convincing them that she was someone who could be trusted in providing a safe and loving home for their child.

Before she followed through with her plan, however, she put her own child up for adoption and sent her away.

"It was a choice that she made," Vale said. "She had options. She could have worked through. But instead what she does is to farm her own child out and opt for the easy money that she seemed to be able to make."

"As Amelia chose to go into the baby farming business," Rattle said. "She was maybe able to travel around here, there and everywhere adopting babies so it made sense for her daughter to be out of the way."

Three years after her first husband George died, Amelia remarried. His name was William Dyer, a brewers laborer from Bristol. They had two children together, Mary Ann aka Polly and William Samuel.

Amelia eventually left William, however, as the latter lost his job and offered little in the way of finances.

Strapped for cash, Amelia decided to dispense with the heavy cost of letting the babies die through neglect and starvation. So after each child was born she promptly murdered them, thus incurring a windfall of profits.

"Baby farmers used different methods," Klansman said. "Some of which are less palatable than others."

"Quite often she would suffocate babies at birth," Rattle said. "Smothering the baby the moment its head came out, before it turned blue as that would be a sign that it had taken its first breath. (She made) it would look like a stillbirth so the death certificate would all be above board."

When her daughter Polly asked why so many babies came and disappeared, Amelia described herself as the "angel maker."

"I'm sending little children to Jesus," Amelia said. "Because he wanted them far more than their mothers did."

"Cold," Alan McCormick of New Scotland Yard said in describing Amelia. "Those kids meant nothing to her. It was just a means of getting money."

It can be argued, however, that once Amelia got a taste of killing she did it more for the power than the money and greed.

"The actual killing of the child," Holmes said. "Watching the child peacefully to some degree die. It parallels perhaps seeing her mother pass away where she felt an almost God-like power over these children that she had decided were going to go to their maker."

AROUSING SUSPICION

"Amelia was already aware of the fact that this was not going to be about her helping children," forensic psychologist David Holmes said. "This was going to be a fairly cruel and anti-mothering act that would be carried out in order to gain all of this money."

Amelia successfully avoided police involvement until 1879, a good ten years into her murderous ways. A doctor became suspicious about the number of child deaths he had been called in to certify under Amelia's care.

"The inquests were held in Somerset," Vale said. "And they're (the police) pretty certain that the babies have died as a direct result of neglect and opium overdose. But they can't prove it. And interestingly, she gets off with a six months sentence with hard labor."

Without a coroner that was able to rule completely against her, Amelia would have undoubtedly been executed by hanging.

"Its incredibly really," Rattle said. "That she only got six months. And there was one example, we read of a chap who got twelve months for stealing a piece of bacon."

Amelia took the punishment hard, becoming an emotional wreck during her jail stay. She resumed her business, however, as soon as she was released.

"In the long term," Holmes reasoned. "It mostly would have served as a very hard lesson in forensic awareness that she wasn't gonna get caught again. And there was no way she was going to leave any evidence which had been the problem in leading up to her capture."

She was sent to mental hospitals for supposed mental illness and suicidal ideations but these seemed to be well-timed acts. From her experience of working in an asylum, Amelia knew the tricks of the trade in order to make her stay an easy one.

"I don't think Amelia Dyer was insane," said Vale. "I think she was a very bad person who deliberately committed murder for profit."

Amelia had both an alcohol and substance abuse problem, using on a regular basis as she began her killings once again.

"Certainly the drugs would have had an impact on her," Richards said. "On her mental state. Maybe induced this complete detachment from reality."

"A long term laudanum habit," Vale concurred. "Will lead to periods of depression. It can lead to mood swings even when you're not under the influence. I think it also exacerbates any underlying mental health issues."

RETURNING TO BABY FARMING

In 1884, British society took a much harder line against baby farming and any sign of neglect or abuse would be reported.

"She definitely changes her modus operandi at this point (after 1884)," Vale said. "She's beginning to murder these children."

In 1890, Amelia took on the care of the illegitimate baby of a governess. She had begun targeting the babies of the more affluent because of the larger amounts of money involved. The higher up the social class the woman was, however, the more risk was involved as the woman may have means to question and come after Amelia.

"This was a young governess who fell in love with the young master of the house that she worked in and had got pregnant," Rattle said. "She was left on her own and she responds to an advert, gets in touch with Amelia Dyer and moves in with her. Amelia was able to gain the trust of this woman as with many others, so much so that the governess was persuaded to leave her baby in the care of Amelia once it was born."

The governess, however, returned to visit her baby months later and immediately became suspicious that the child she was given was not hers. She stripped the baby to see if a birth mark was present on one of its hips. It wasn't and the governess immediately informed the authorities.

The police, however, could never pin Amelia down.

"She managed to put them off time and time again by sending them on wild goose chases," Rattle said. "She said she had sent them to a couple that moved here...that moved there."

Amelia continued to move from town to town but still found herself being stalked by the governess who wouldn't give up.

"She did feel hounded," Richards said. "I'm sure that would have had an impact on her. She would have felt that pressure."

Amelia then feigned another nervous breakdown and a doctor was brought in. "The birds are telling me to do it! The birds are telling me to do it!" she would cry out, forcing the doctor to send her to an asylum.

"She was a very clever lady," Holmes said. "With the police getting close to her and she needed to lose herself and what better place to go than somewhere like that (a mental asylum)."

Her mental illness continued on unabated as she drank two bottles of laudanum in an attempted suicide. Her long term use of opium, however, allowed her to build up the tolerance necessary to survive.

"Amelia would be drawn to the idea of self-medicating," Holmes said. "Possibly seeing it as a route, a means to ease the situation, make it even easier for her to put up with what she was doing."

"She took it (opium) on a regular basis," Richards said. "She took it almost daily so she was an addict. So that would induce a form of state from her mentally where she would be detached from reality and I think that was part of her coping mechanism to detach from the reality of what she was doing."

After that close call and subsequent hospital release, Amelia resumed baby farming and murder.

"Her mental breakdowns were very short lived," Richards noted. "She would be out of sorts for a period of time that get it all back together again. To me that would say there isn't a mental illness there."

A CLEVER KILLER

She wised up to doing things on the books and decided to stop getting doctors to issue death certificates. Amelia decided to kill and bury the bodies herself. In order to do this, she would have to be a killer on the run as inevitably the mothers would come back seeking to reclaim their children or check on their welfare. Amelia took her family to different cities to escape suspicion as soon as things got too hot. She would use a series of different aliases and rename her businesses.

"Amelia committed what many serial killers do," Holmes explained. "The mistake of accelerating and being over enthusiastic. Either for reasons that she was enjoying the process or quite simply greed was driving her over the edge."

Baby farming began to gain the attention and compassion of the British ruling class, however. They asked why if they had laws for the prevention of the cruelty of animals then why didn't there laws protecting children. With the arrest and hanging of Margaret Waters (another baby farming killer) and the fleeing Dyer, Amelia's colleagues were going downhill fast and perhaps she thought her time was limited.

By 1893, Amelia had another breakdown but was released from the Wells mental asylum. This would be the last time she would be hospitalized. She moved to

Caversham, Berkshire with a woman named Jane "Granny" Smith who didn't know of Amelia's exploits.

"She befriends an old lady named Jane Smith," Vale said. "She's widowed and resigned to spend her last days in the workhouse. Amelia seduces her with stories of rescuing the unwanted infants. Of nursing them. And it's a very, very seductive image. And Jane Smith buys into it, wholesale."

Her daughter Mary Ann aka Polly and her husband Arthur Palmer came along as well.

The group moved to 45 Kensington Road, Reading Berkshire in that same year. Amelia had the perfect front. She coached Jane Smith to call her "mother" in front of prospective clients while Amelia would call her "Granny."

A ruse to project a mother-daughter image and put the guards down of the pregnant young women.

"Jane Smith didn't get the life she was promised at all," Rattle said. "She was treated as no more than a servant really. She was made to look after the children, to clean the house."

Amelia then puts her adoptions into overdrive. The babies come in and out of the house with such rapidity that old lady Jane Smith doesn't even learn their names.

Eyewitnesses later claimed that there were six infants a day coming to and from the house daily.

THE MURDERS CONTINUE

The advertisement in the "Miscellaneous" column of the Bristol Times & Mirror newspaper was poignant.

In January of 1896 a popular barmaid named Evelina Marmon gave birth to a daughter out of wedlock. She named the baby Doris and she sought immediately to have it adopted. She placed an ad in the "Miscellaneous" section of the Bristol Times & Mirror newspaper.

"*Wanted, respectable woman to take young child.*" Marmon intended to go back to work and hoped to eventually reclaim her child.

Evelina was a God-fearing farmer's daughter who left the farm for city life. She found work as a barmaid in the saloon of the Plough Hotel, an old coaching inn. She was buxom with blonde hair and had a vibrant personality. She had plenty of suitors and became pregnant by one of the male patrons who left her deserted.

Evelina knew she could not bring up the baby on her own.

She would have to find a foster home for little Doris - to have her "adopted out", in the language of the time - go back to work and hope in time to be able to reclaim her child.

Next to her own ad was an advertisement that read *"Married couple with no family would adopt healthy child, nice country home. Terms, £10".*

Marmon answered the ad which was addressed to a "Mrs. Harding", an alias of Amelia. A few days later Amelia wrote back, saying *"I should be glad to have a dear little baby girl, one I could bring up and call my own. We are plain, homely people, in fairly good circumstances. I don't want a child for money's sake, but for company and home comfort... Myself and my husband are dearly fond of children. I have no child of my own. A child with me will have a good home and a mother's love. It is just lovely here, heatlhy and pleasant. There is an orchard opposite our front door."*

Evelina was assured that she could visit whenever she wished.

"Rest assured I will do my duty by that dear child. I will be a mother, as far as lies in my power."

"It is just lovely here, healthy and pleasant. There is an orchard opposite our front door."

Evelina tried to negotiate a weekly fee for the care of Doris but Amelia wanted a substantial one-time fee to be paid upfront. Evelina, seemingly with no other choice, agreed to pay the £10, and a week later "Mrs Harding" arrived in Cheltenham.

Evelina was surprised that Amelia aka "Mrs. Harding" was old (59 years) and heavy set (over 210 lbs). She remained reluctant at first but gave in as the elderly woman immediately showed her Doris some affection, covering her with a shawl.

Evelina gave the old lady a cardboard box of clothes she had prepared – nappies, chemises, petticoats, frocks, nightgowns, and a powder box. She also enclosed the money and received a signed receipt from "Mrs.Harding."

She accompanied her baby daughter and her eventual killer to Cheltenham station then on to Gloucester. Evelina stood there crying through the hot steam on the platform as the 5:20 p.m train took her baby away.

When Evelina returned home, she described herself as "a broken woman."

Days later, she received a letter from "Mrs. Harding" offering her assurance that all was well with her daughter. Evelina wrote back but received no replies afterward.

Amelia told Evelina that she would be going to Reading but lied. She traveled to 76 Mayo Road, Willesden, London where her daughter Mary Ann was staying. Amelia then took some white edging tape and wrapped it around the baby's neck, making a strangling knot. The baby did not die immediately.

"I used to like to watch them with the tape around their neck," Amanda said. "But it was soon all over with them."

"The idea of strangling and using the tape may make it seem almost symbolical or bizarre to ourselves," Holmes said. "But in terms of criminal awareness she was aware of the fact that if she tried to suffocate a baby its not always absolutely certain that the baby is dead."

The mother and daughter team wrapped the baby up with a napkin. They kept the clothes that Evelina gave her and hoped to sell it to a pawnbroker. Amelia used some of the money to pay the rent to her landlady and gave the woman a pair of child's boots as a present for her own little girl.

The following day, April 1st of 1896, a young boy named Harry Simmons was taken to the Mayo Road residence. Amelia had no spare white edging tape available and used the tape from Doris' corpse to strangle the year old boy.

The next day both bodies were rolled into a carpet bag, their corpses stacked one on top of the other. Bricks were added inside for additional weight. Amelia headed back toward Reading, taking the bus to Paddington and then the train. She dragged the carpet bag through the streets until she reached the River Thames. She had a secluded spot at Caversham Lock and she forced the carpet bag through the railing and didn't leave until she heard it splash into the waters below.

She didn't know she had a witness as a man passed, hurrying on his way home calling out "Good night."

A SHOCKING DISCOVERY

Ironically, only days before the dumping of the bodies a package was fished out of the Thames by a bargeman. This package was the work of Amelia as she had not weighed it down adequately. It contained the body of a baby girl named Helena Fry. With only a small police force available in Reading, a Constable Anderson made a significant discovery. He found a label from Temple Meads Station, Bristol and he used microscopic analysis of the wrapping paper. He found a faintly legible name. A "Mrs.Thomas" and an address.

The address of Amelia Dyer.

The police immediately placed Amelia's home under surveillance. They did enough research on Amelia and knew that she would "disappear" if she thought she was under suspicion. So they decided they would be better served if they would use a young woman as a decoy to secure a meeting with Amelia and discuss the prospect of using her "adoptive services."

On April 3rd, while Amelia was waiting on the decoy to arrive, she answered the door to a police raid. The smell of decomposing bodies radiated throughout her home but no human remains were found. The police found other evidence, however, such as the white edging tape, telegrams describing adoption arrangements, pawn tickets for children's clothing, receipts for newspaper ads and letters from distraught mothers asking about the welfare of their child.

The police determined that in the few months Amelia had been in Reading at least twenty children had been placed into her care. She had been preparing to move again, this time to the town of Somerset.

Amelia was arrested on April 4th, three days after the murders of Doris Marmon and Harry Simmons. The Thames River was searched and six more bodies were discovered, including Doris and Harry.

Each child had been strangled with the seamstress white tape and Amelia later told police that "was how you could tell it was one of mine."

Eleven days later, Evelina Marmon had been contacted by police as they found her name in items found in Amelia's home. Distraught, she came to identify her daughter's remains.

THE TRIAL OF A KILLER

An inquest was held a month later. Amelia's daughter Mary Ann and her husband Arthur were not charged as there was no direct evidence that they were her accomplices. Arthur was set free because of a confession handwritten by Amelia. She wrote:

Sir will you kindly grant me the favour of presenting this to the magistrates on Saturday the 18th instant I have made this statement out, for I may not have the opportunity then I must relieve my mind I do know and I feel my days are numbered on this earth but I do feel it is an awful thing drawing innocent people into trouble I do know I shal have to answer before my Maker in Heaven for the awful crimes I have committed but as God Almighty is my judge in Heaven a on Hearth neither my daughter Mary Ann Palmer nor her husband Alfred Ernest Palmer I do most solemnly declare neither of them had any thing at all to do with it, they never knew I contemplated doing such a wicked thing until it was to late I am speaking the truth and nothing but the truth as I hope to be forgiven, I myself and I alone must stand before my Maker in Heaven to give an answer for it all witnes my hand
    Amelia Dyer.

— April 16, 1896

On May 22nd, 1896, Amelia appeared in court and pleaded guilty to the murder of Doris Marmon. Her family and friends testified that they had their own suspicions about Amelia and spoke of times that she evaded discovery. A man came forth claiming he had seen and spoken to Amelia as she had disposed of two bodies at Caversham Lock proved key to the prosecution.

Amelia used insanity as a defense, offering her stays in mental asylums as proof of her instability. The prosecution, however, argued that her symptoms were well-rehearsed actions to avoid suspicion as both of her hospital stays coincided with times that Amelia felt her murders would be discovered.

The jury took four and a half minutes to find her guilty. Amelia then spent three weeks in her condemned cell, filling five journals with her confessions. A chaplain visited her the night before her execution and asked if she had anything to confess. She offered him her journals, asking "isn't this enough?"

Amelia was then subpoenaed to appear as a witness in her daughter's own trial for murder which was set for a week after her own execution date. The court ruled, however, that Amelia became "legally dead" after she was sentenced and her testimony would be inadmissible.

On the day of her execution, Amelia discovered that the charges against her daughter had been dropped.

On June 10th, 1896, Amelia Dyer was hanged by James Billington at Newgate Prison. Asked on the scaffold if she had anything to say, she said "I have nothing to say."

URBAN LEGEND?

It remains unknown as to why Amelia's daughter Mary Ann aka Polly was never convicted. Her own daughter provided the majority of the testimony that procured the conviction of her mother but nothing is said about her own involvement.

And the baby murders did not stop after Amelia's death.

Two years after her execution, railroad workers inspecting carriages found a parcel tied up with a string inside a siding on the Plymouth express.

Inside was a three-week old baby girl. The infant was shivering and wet...but alive.

A little research showed that the baby was the child of a widow named Jane Hill. Hill had given the baby to a woman named "Mrs. Stewart" for the one time fee of £12.

"The little one would have a good home and a parent's love and care," Mrs. Stewart had written, her prose eerilly echoing that of Amelia Dyer. "Mrs. Stewart" had picked up the baby at Plymouth and dumped her on the next train.

The conjecture was that "Mrs. Stewart" was none other than Polly, Amelia's daughter.

SATAN'S DAUGHTER

THE TRUE STORY OF NATASHA CORNETT

99

TRISH SAMUELSON

Natasha Cornett was born January 26th, 1979 in Pikeville, Kentucky.

Pikeville is located in the foothills of the Appalachian mountains. It is a mining town with most of its inhabitants devoutly religious.

"It's very beautiful scenery to grow up in," Cornett said. "But it's a suffocating place to live."

Born poor, Natasha was the product of an affair between her mother Madonna Wallen and her biological father, a police officer named Roger Burgess.

Her mother then left her husband, Ed Wallen, and raised Natasha alone. They lived in a trailer in Pikeville, Kentucky.

"She had energy to burn," her mother said. "She liked to draw. To read. She liked dogs and babies."

SCHOOL LIFE

Natasha was a good student in elementary school, behaving well and getting good grades. She seemed to be on the right path until one morning she found her mother laying unconscious. Madonna Wallen had overdosed on prescription drugs.

"My momma is on the bed naked," Cornett recalled. "With a bottle of pills laying next to her. I didn't know she was dying. It messed with me."

Around this time, Cornett's life began a downward spiral. She began suffering from anorexia. Then drugs. Then she began engaging in acts of self-mutilation, cutting her arms to "relieve her pain."

"Natasha started to engage in those acts as a means of getting control," forensic psychologist Roberta Nixon said. "She can control her diet. She can control her anger, or so she thinks, by cutting herself. She can control how she feels by doing drugs. Having a dim-witted mother certainly didn't help things either."

At one point, Natasha had lost over thirty pounds because of her anorexia as well as having over seventy cuts on her arms.

"I started cutting because I started going through a rough time with my mom," Natasha said. "It was a release."

"I don't know where that pain comes from," Natasha's mother, Madonna Wallen said. "She just says she has to do it to take away her pain."

In later court testimony, however, Wallen would admit to a history of physical abuse with her daughter.

"I used a belt one time and the buckles slipped from my hand," Wallen said. "And it hit her on the back of the leg. But it made a bruise on her."

Wallen later said that there was sexual abuse of Natasha by her husband whom she originally believed to be Natasha's father.

"Natasha had a really bad upbringing," C. Berkeley Bell, the District Attorney General for Tennessee said. "Lot of hard times. She came from a very dysfunctional family. Hard time in school. Was an outcast. Was ostracized by her classmates."

HIGH SCHOOL DROPOUT

Natasha entered high school but dropped out before her freshman year was complete. Her best friend was Karen Howell who would later be part of the "Wild Bunch" that Cornett would lead on a killing spree.

"Karen was my life raft," Natasha said. "She was the only person that understood me and let me be me. She knew my pain. She went through the same stuff."

Like Natasha, Karen had a dysfunctional family. Her father was an abusive alcoholic and her mother had a nervous breakdown. She came from a strict, religious family with her mother forcing her to stand on a Bible when she misbehaved. She was also bipolar.

"They were like two peas in a pod," Nixon said. "But in court interviews Natasha seems to more of a realization of what took place that night. Karen remained a petulant teenager, sullen and angry. Natasha was the better talker of the two so Karen followed her lead.

BIPOLAR DISORDER

Natasha was eventually diagnosed with bipolar disorder and in one episode had to be hospitalized at the Ridge Treatment Center in Lexington, KY. She had to leave the hospital after eleven days, however, as that was all the time the state health benefits would allow.

"Bipolar disease is brutal and even more so for people in low income circumstances," Nixon said. "It is extremely hard to treat. The amazing thing here is that she was only hospitalized for eleven days. After that, she doesn't appear to have gone through any kind of outpatient treatment program aside from an aborted session with a counselor. With people like Natasha, they need medication to keep their anxiety and impulses under control. Without it, anything can happen and anything will happen."

Natasha's mother began to see the rapid decline in her emotional state. Her choice of clothing would be reflect her mood and growing anger.

"From the seventh grade," Wallen said. "She just started changing. The big baggy pants. The rope with the emblems hanging. Everybody thought it was weird."

"I started drinking and smoking and associating with people that were weird," Natasha said. "You don't have to be perfect around them."

Natasha sought acceptance and eventually found it in the Goth subculture. Still, with the rapid mood shifts and change in dress, Natasha's own mother insists that there are three versions of Natasha.

"There is the sweet, caring girl," Wallen said. "There is the girl who would do anything for her friends, and there is a dark side that likes to play on a Oujia board, do seances and play vampire games."

MARRIAGE

At the age of seventeen, Natasha married Stephen Cornett. It was no ordinary ceremony, however. The bride and groom wore black and dog collars.

"We'd been friends for awhile," Natasha said. "It seemed like the logical thing to do."

The union only lasted a couple of months. Steven left without warning, abandoning Natasha. The dissolution of the marriage caused Natasha to spiral further into depression.

"It was awful," Natasha said. "I just kinda caved in on myself."

Natasha then fully immersed herself in the Goth subculture even further. She donned black clothing and listened intently to the dark, depressing music. She would pierce her eyebrows and lips with safety pins as well as use black lipstick and nail polish.

"For most kids," Nixon said. "The Goth culture is a way to rebel. To control their own image. It is a relatively harmless phase for most involved. They're young. They act out. Then they grow out of it. For some kids, however, like Natasha, it is more than that. She's disturbed to begin with and wants to take it beyond the dark music and black get-ups and really wants to do harm to someone. She realized that the Goth culture was a way to make people afraid of her. This is how she would gain power. She could control people by being their 'darkness consultant.'"

NATASHA THE VAMPIRE

She became a self-described "vampire" and named her black dog "Malkavian" after the vampires in her favorite vampire fantasy board game as well as collecting all of Anne Rice's vampire novels.

"She was a dark soul who'd give you the willies," a local teen said in describing her.

Natasha covered the walls of her bedroom in her trailer with numerous dark messages including "I hate the world" as well as drawing inverted crosses.

"Tasha would start hearing voices," Wallen said. "Talking to people on the Oujia board. Her and Karen fed on each other. You know. It just kept getting worse. She wanted away from all the people that called her 'freak.'"

Her drug use and drinking increased but she was able to attract a group of friends, most of whom looked up to her. The group consisted of three girls. The petite Karen Howell and the overweight, awkward Crystal Sturgill.

Sturgill was molested by her step-father and had been kicked out of her home. She needed a place to stay and hooked up with Karen and Natasha.

The threesome would go around the sleepy Kentucky town, spray painting pentagrams, the satanic number 666 and inverted crosses across the walls of buildings and homes.

"They were all sort of drop outs," reporter Bill Jones said. "Who fell through the cracks in school. They dressed in Gothic fashion, black clothing. Black make-up. Looks Satanic, if you're looking for Satanic that's what might come to mind."

"Everything that we did," Natasha said. "Was very destructive but also self-destructive. Nothing was done to harm anybody but ourselves."

Natasha began spelling her name backwards, 'Ah-Satan', spray painting it across the walls of the town.

"She used the name to intimidate," Dixon said. "In an odd way, that was part of her charm. She was more 'out there' than the impressionable kids in her town. She held sway over Karen Howell and Crystal Sturgill, both of whom were looking for someone they could look up to. So while Natasha was an outcast at school she was able to assemble other outcasts and cast them under her spell. She became the devil of choice to worship."

The gang carried around two books with them, *The Book of Black Magic* and the *Complete Book of Magic and Witchcraft*. The three girls would go to motel rooms or Natasha's mother's trailer to hang out, drink alcohol and each other's blood. They would also engage in seances and Satanic rituals they would read about in books.

"When it comes to the occult," Dixon said. "Most young people just dabble around with it. In the case of Natasha and her gang, however, she led them over the edge. They were dumb kids out looking for kicks and she pushed them into something that they probably would not have gotten involved in had it not been for her own dark compulsions."

ROAD TRIP TO HELL

"We're going to start armageddon," Natasha informed one of her friends. "I hate, therefore I am" became her mantra.

Natasha and the "Wild Bunch" decided to go on a road trip to New Orleans. They were obsessed with the vampire books of Anne Rice and thought about the prospect of meeting her. Talks began and the entire group wanted to leave the small town of Pikeville behind.

"All I could think of was I need out," Natasha said. "I need out. I need out. I need out. I can't breathe, I need out."

The group of girls were now joined by some equally nefarious young men. The first is Joe Risner who is Karen's boyfriend and at twenty years old, the oldest in the group. Risner, never knew his own father and was known as the quiet, introverted type. He wanted to impressed Karen but was insecure as his love interest seemed more infatuated with Natasha then with him.

Edward Dean Mullins was nineteen and the only one from the group that comes from an intact family that goes to church. He is struggling with self-esteem issues, however, as women reject him until he meets Natasha. James Bryant is fourteen but seemingly the most volatile of the "Wild Bunch". His mother has abandoned him and left him alone with an alcoholic father. Natasha and Karen met him on a street corner and picked him up because they thought he looked "cool." Mostly likely, they saw him as someone the could use to do their dirty work.

"I had been friends with Joe for awhile," Natasha said. "Joe was dating Karen. Crystal needed a place to stay and she was friends with Dean (Mullins)."

Jason was the last entry into the "Wild Bunch." It was apparent, however, that he and Natasha didn't always see eye to eye. According to detectives, Jason was not as "controllable" as others in Natasha's group.

"Jason didn't make a huge impact on me," Natasha said. "He seemed dangerous. Like people pretend to be bad. I thought that was his hook. He was the 'bad boy.'"

Natasha's mother's trailer would be their primary hangout where they would drink, do drugs and later plot out their killing spree.

"Prior to leaving (for the road trip)," Bell said. "The defendants would watch 'Natural Born Killers.' That movie depicts individuals who are carefree, killing people. There don't appear to be from that movie, any consequences (to violence). They may have felt that there were not going to be any consequences for their actions. I really don't know what it takes for a group of people to take on that mentality of murder. They had no concept of tomorrow. Or consequences. And they just don't care."

The members of the gang become increasingly excited as they discuss the prospects of what will take place on their killing spree. Finally, they have some excitement in their boring, despondent lives with Natasha at the head.

"She seemed to be the leader of the group," Jones said. "And someone in the group said 'we're going to make headlines.'"

MOTEL SEVEN PIT STOP

The group piled into Risner's mother's car, a compact Chevy Citation. Before they would hit the highway, they rented out room number seven at the Colley Motel in Pikeville. Despite Natasha's apparent disdain for Jason, the young fourteen year old had cut Natasha's initials into his arm that night at the motel. The group then attempted to burn the satanic numbers 666 into the motel carpet with candle wax.

They would then begin their self-mutilation ritual.

"Me and Karen started cutting," Natasha said. "And at first, it was just to cut. Then I wanted to die. I thought eventually if I cut myself so many times I would just bleed out. Mostly it was just me and Karen drinking each others blood. We just didn't do seances."

Crystal maintains that they were not part of a vampire cult or nor did they worship Satan. "We dressed in black and we'd stand out. And we did self-multilation. We were the freaks, the outcasts."

"We were trying to find answers, " Crystal said during in interview with Campus Life. "We all had been to church. It didn't provide answers. We were interested in Wicca, books on witches and spells. We were anarchists."

"They wanted to go to New Orleans," Natasha said. "Because that was the only place I was familiar with. And I said I wouldn't go back down there without some kind of protection."

Natasha was referring to the fact that she claimed to be raped in New Orleans although no charges were filed.

The motel owner, Jim Cochran, said that he rented out the room to Risner and described him as "polite and courteous". Risner, who also wore the Goth black make-up was described by detectives as "lanky and long-haired." A week before their killing spree, Natasha was in a Pikeville grocery store where she led Risner around by a dog chain fastened to a collar around his neck.

The group started a fire in the motel room and they were worried the manager would call the cops.

"Karen had just gotten into trouble," Natasha said. "And she didn't want to go back to juvenile. Jason just got out of juvenile and he didn't want to go back. And I was ready to run away at any given moment so it just kinda came together. We were all going to run away."

The group then vandalized and burglarized other Colley Motel rooms during their stay. They stole a television set and several pairs of work boots.

ROUTE 666

The group of disaffected youth drove to Forty-Acre Field, a remote campground where other teens would hang out. They started a campfire then at some point that night or early in the morning they burglarized two homes in a town called Paintsville. It was there they stole two semi-automatic handguns.

They thought about performing a carjacking as Joe's mother's Chevy Citation kept overheating. Nonetheless, they went onto U.S. Highway 23 south into Virginia.

The group was ticketed for speeding in Gate City, Virginia on April 6th but were allowed to continue on.

"Based on the evidence of what their stated purpose was," Bell said. "The night before they left. They were preparing to leave Pikeville. Go across the country. Robbing and killing people."

The group then drove into a used car lot and tried unsuccessfully to hot wire a vehicle.

They kept driving and an hour later, they stopped at the Interstate Highway 81 rest stop in Greeneville, Tennessee.

"Karen needed to pee," Natasha said.

Tragedy would ensue as the group came upon the Lillelid family at a truck stop in Greeneville,

THE LILLELID FAMILY

Thirty-four year old Norwegian Vidar Lillelid, his twenty-eight year old wife Delfina, their six year old daughter Tabitha and two year old son Peter were having lunch on a park bench.

Vidar, who worked as a hotel bellman, had taken his family to a religious convention in Johnson City. They were on their way home to Nashville. He had been in the USA for ten years. His wife, Delfina was a native of New Jersey but had parents who had immigrated from Honduras. The two had married in 1989 and moved to Knoxville four years earlier from Miami because they wanted a nice place to raise their two children. The two were described as "devoutly faithful" and "humble" by those who knew them.

"The Jehovah's Witnesses were having a convention abut thirty miles north," Jones recalled. "They had been to that convention and they were going home. Jehovah Witnesses are known for being active in trying to recruit new members. They leave pamphlets and that sort of thing. That may have been the worst thing they could have done."

"I think they were doing a little proselytizing there," Bell said. "It was just part of their religion that they go out and try and talk to people. They saw the defendant's unusual appearance. They may have though that they needed some discussion about the Lord."

Vidar and Delfina approached the group and asked if they believed in God. Natasha spoke for the everyone, saying she dd not believe in God, as he had never come to her aid when she prayed as a child.

"The whole scenario just drips with tragic irony," Dixon said. "On one hand, we have the Lillelid family. They are sweet and naïve. They are following the dictates of their church to go out and invite as many members as they can for their church. Then there are these cult members who a diametrically opposed viewpoint. They have their own beliefs. Only theirs are something far more sinister."

KIDNAPPING AT GUNPOINT

According to Natasha, it was Joe who initiated the kidnapping of the family.

"It was when Joe said he wanted to converse with Vidar about his religious beliefs," Natasha said. "That just brought up red flags, because Joe was not a religious man. I tried to convince him (Joe) that we should just leave and get on our own way. Every step that he took, I was there trying to prevent it."

Natasha stated that it was never their intent to rob and kill the Lillelids. She became alarmed with Joe who went back to his car and got his gun. Then after conversing with Jason, Joe pulled the gun out on the Lillelids.

Detectives confirmed that Joe Risner admitted that he was the one that pulled the gun. Natasha remained steadfast in her own statement that she tried to stop Joe.

"He was like 'nothing is gonna happen,'" Natasha said. "'We just need your car.' All I could do was just look at them and apologize."

Vidar immediately offered his keys and wallet, pleading for the killers to not harm his family.

"They put them in their respective cars and took off," Bell said. "They got off the Interstate. Just a few miles down the road."

"I didn't think that the people that I was around could actually do anything bad," Natasha said. "Even Jason. I thought I could stop something."

Detectives found out otherwise, however. During interviews with the other members of the group, they believed that Natasha was the instigator. She was the one that members of the group thought could "draw on demons" and was the driving force behind the robbery.

Joseph Risner forced the family into the Citation. They drove along until they reach a remote area.

"It's a dead end, gravel, one lane road," Jones said. "They go down the end of that road and force the people out of the car."

The family is terrified. Vidar continued to plead for mercy. Young Peter is clinging to his mother's leg, his arms wrapped tight around her waist.

"This group of very strange looking people is surrounding them and laughing," Bell said. "And they see the weapon."

"I can't imagine what that would have been like," Jones said. "To know that your family was in peril like that."

According to Natasha, it was Risner that pulled the gun on the family but now on the deserted road it was Jason Bryant, the fourteen year old, who held the family at gunpoint.

"All of a sudden Jason pulled the gun up," Natasha said. "All I could see was rage on his face. And Joe walked away from it. He was like, 'I can't do that.' And I was like 'Jason, what are you doing? And he just started cussing. 'Get the fuck outta the way! Get the fuck outta the way! Move! Unless you wanna die, move!

"I got in between Jason and the family to where the gun was pointed at me and tried to convince him to not do that. I begged and I pleaded for what seemed like an eternity for him to stop. When I discovered that there was no stopping him, I begged for at least the children to be saved. He told me that if I didn't move, he would shoot me."

"I don't think I would have moved anyway until he promised and swore to me that he would not harm the children. That's when I moved. I didn't think that I could do anything to prevent it if I was dead."

During the testimony, Natasha, Risner and Karen Howell said that Bryant did the shooting. Bryant, however, said that Risner and Edward Dean Mullins fired the shots and later forced him to take the blame.

Gunpowder was found on Mullins, however. The detectives and prosecuting attorney believed that the entire group somehow were involved in the shootings as over seventeen shots were fired.

"If you wanted to be a member of this group," Bell said. "You had to participate in this ritualistic killing."

"I don't know which (of the family) got shot first," Bell said. "But the rest of them are observing their family being shot."

"The indication was that the children were shot last," Jones said. "The little girl had apparently walked around in her mother's blood. The boy even though he was two years old was shot in the head."

"I didn't watch," Natasha claimed. "I sat in the back of the van and just screamed. Please don't hurt them. Please don't hurt them. Please don't hurt them. Jason said 'Stop fucking crying.' He just laughed."

Six year old Tabitha was shot in the head. Peter was being held by his mother as he was shot. Each of the victim was shot in the eye as a 'signature' move.

"The males were shot in the right eye," Bell said. "And the women on the left."

"It was a ritualized killing," Dixon said. "Call it bonding through murder. They would hoop and holler and cheer each other on. "

The group left Risner's mother's car at the scene as it became stuck in the mud. They stole the family's van, the youths took off in the hopes of going to Mexico.

But not before they had dragged the bodies over, lying the four bodies parallel to each other so it appeared like a four-pointed star.

Joe laughed as they drove over the bodies, hearing the crunch of bone under the weight of the van.

THE AFTERMATH

Vidar and Delfina were found dead, tire tracks across their clothing. Tabitha was still alive when found but died en route to the hospital. Two year old Peter was shot in the torso and the eye. Amazingly, the boy survived although he is now blind in one eye and permanently disabled.

"Peter survived," Jones said. "The two year old boy had been shot through the eye with the bullet exiting the side of his head. It didn't kill him. He's disabled by the extent of his injuries. He had difficulty walking and of course, blind in one eye.

The youths showed no remorse after the shooting. People who lived nearby heard gunshots, laughing and shouting as they left the family for dead. The police were called and the Sheriffs discovered the dead bodies of the Lillelid family.

ON THE RUN

"After you witness something that atrocious," Natasha said. "I didn't know what to do."

The group went on the run, altering their plans to go to New Orleans. Instead, they headed to Arizona/Mexico border.

Two days after the shootings, Natasha and her cohorts were arrested by US Customs and Immigration officials in Arizona.

"They had been down into Mexico," Bell said. "And as they were coming back through the computers at the border had not been functioning. So the border could not check on who was coming in and out. But just as that group came back in the computer suddenly started working. And when they put the license tag in the system they got a hit. And they were arrested there in Arizona."

The detectives and defense attorney who dealt with Natasha after the arrest vary widely from her own well-thought versions of what took place that night.

"She was a vampire who worshiped Satan," said an officer who spoke to Natasha after her arrest. "She was on the dark side. Very bitter towards everyone."

Natasha allegedly told her first defense attorney, Eric Conn, that she was 'Satan's Daughter.' The attorney decided to play up that aspect of her defense as he hoped to get her a lenient sentence if she was declared insane.

"After Eric Conn got up in the devil worship and vampirism," Wallen said. "It kept getting worse and worse."

Natasha blames her first lawyer, Conn, for her lackluster defense.

"I don't know why it was me that was picked out of everyone else," Natasha said. "I know he did a lot of damage to me and my case.

"I didn't tell him that I even had any inclination toward that," Natasha recalled. "I knew he was a lawyer wanting to represent me pro bono. At no point had I ever been a satanist. Ever. Once something like that is said. You can't just take it back."

Conn was later replaced by Stacy Street but the damage had been done.

Natasha's current court-appointed attorney stated that "he (Conn) volunteered to represent her, then immediately began negotiating movie rights.

SOUVENIRS OF A KILL

"Each one of these killers," Berkeley said. "Took an individual trophy from their victims. And kept it attached to a chain or a wallet."

Karen Howell took Vidar's social security card and Tabitha's 'Hello Kitty' merchandise. Natasha took Tabitha's social security card and her wallet. Sturgill had taken the keys to the Lillelid home all for souvenirs.

DEATH PENALTY?

"We were very concerned that the proof might focus on the juveniles as being the shooters," Bell said. "Juveniles can't get the death penalty. And if they can't get the death penalty we were concerned that no one else would get the death penalty either. What we reached was an agreement that we'd have a hearing."

A media circus followed the trial as an angry mob descended upon the teenagers as they entered the courtroom.

"Someone yelled that I was Charles Manson's daughter," recalled Sturgill.

In the trial, all six defendants had different stories as to how events took place that night and who pulled the trigger.

"It is my position that it was part of an initiation," Bell said. "That everybody had to participate in the shooting."

"Natasha clearly was the ring leader in all of the killings here," Dixon said. "She was the most articulate and confident of the group. The young men in the group were all shy types, eager from some female validation, with the possible exception of Jason who was a budding psychopath. But again, he was a dim-witted fourteen year old pitted against a smooth-talker in Natasha. Sturgill and Howell looked up to Natasha in their own ways as well. Sturgill was social awkward, overweight. She finally found people she could call friends and would do whatever they said. And Karen would not become violent on her own. These individuals were all like that, they could be violent but needed someone to light the fuse. And Natasha struck the match for everyone.

CONVICTION

Natasha was convicted on March 13th, 1998 with the five other youths. She reached a plea bargain where she plead guilty to all of the charges to avoid the death penalty.

In her court testimony, Natasha maintained that she was not the shooter of the four victims. She kept asserting that she tried to prevent the deaths of the Lillelid family members.

All of the defendants were sentenced to three life terms plus twenty-five years without the possibility of parole.

"She wasn't the shooter," Natasha's mother said, maintaining her daughter's innocence. "She got the same thing as the shooter."

PRISON LIFE

Natasha is housed at a prison in Nashville. She has earned her GED and her mother

Madonna claims that her daughter serves as a "mentor to fellow inmates as they work to earn their GED."

"I was a teacher's aide for about a year," Natasha said during a newspaper interview.

Her troubled times continued, however, as on August of 24th 2001, she and death row inmate Christa Pike allegedly attacked a fellow prisoner named Patricia Jones.

They tried to strangle Jones to death with a shoe string after all three were placed in a holding cell with Natasha during a fire alarm.

Pike was on death row for torturing and beating a woman to death when they were Job Corps students in 1995.

Another inmate, the twenty-year old Jennifer Szostecki started the fire which created confusion during the fire alarm. This allowed Christa Pike to gain access to Patricia Jones.

Jones allegedly teased Pike about her upcoming execution.

"All she does is snitch on me and stab me in the back," Pike said during a phone call with her mother.

Natasha allegedly struggled with Jones before Pike came from behind and started to choke Jones with the shoe strings from a hiking boot. Natasha was Pike's friend and Szostecki's "girlfriend."

Letters filed in criminal court show Szostecki's obsession with Natasha.

"I love you," Sozstecki wrote. "I hate you. I miss you. I want you. I need you."

Pike was later charged with attempted murder while there was insufficient evidence to charge Natasha.

"I expected big women with shanks and stuff like that," Natasha said of her time in prison. "You know, like that typical prison scene that you would see in a movie. But it's not like that. You just get up, go to meals, have an hour out for recreational purposes and watch television and read."

PETER LILLELID

Peter Lillelid would be the subject of a custody battle between his USA based relatives and his aunt in Sweden. His aunt and uncle from Sweden won custody and Peter was sent to be in their care.

They kept him shielded from the media and he does not like to read the accounts of what happened to his parents and sister.